Contents

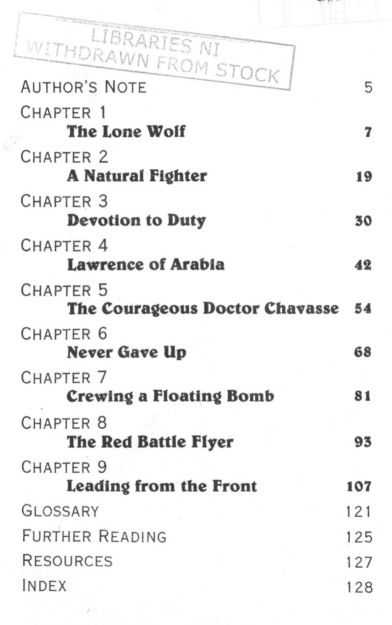

Author's Note

Truth really can be stranger than fiction, and more exciting, astonishing and compelling as well. I hope you will agree that these nine true stories from World War I prove the point.

They feature soldiers, sailors, airmen and civilians from both sides but what links them is that they all record acts of incredible daring, resolve, bravery and compassion. The stories have been compiled from lots of different sources, including previously published accounts, letters and diaries. I spent many fascinating days in museum and library archives, talking to historians and receiving kind assistance from experts and relatives.

I hope you find reading the stories as interesting and inspiring as I found researching and writing them.

Clive

Clive Gifford

Chapter 1

The Lone Wolf

When World War I started, flying was still in its infancy and few military chiefs knew how to make the best use of aircraft. At this stage, planes were mainly used for reconnaissance – to observe the enemy's fortifications and any movements of their troops. Then both sides started to fit machine guns to their aircraft so that they could attempt to attack the other side's 'spotter' planes.

Gradually, specialist planes, designed to bomb targets or shoot down enemy aircraft, appeared. Famous fighter planes of World War I included the Red Baron's Fokker triplane and the Sopwith triplane. But most were two-winged biplanes, like the Nieuport Scout piloted by a young

Nottinghamshire man who – in a short space of time – became Britain's most celebrated flying ace of the war. A quiet, isolated person, a 'lone wolf' in the air, his name was Albert Ball.

◆ ◆ ◆

The small, flimsy aircraft that nineteen-year-old Albert Ball was piloting suddenly dropped over 300 metres. He struggled with the aircraft's controls but was powerless to prevent it plummeting towards the ground. At a speed of over 160 kilometres per hour, Ball's aircraft thudded into the ground, knocking him out.

Coming round, Ball climbed out of the aircraft's mangled cockpit. It didn't concern him that he could have been killed. But what did upset him was the state of his aircraft. It was wrecked – nothing more than matchwood. He had been building up his flying hours as a trainee pilot in the Royal Flying Corps when strong winds had made his craft fall like a stone. In a letter to his parents, Ball claimed, 'I would much rather have smashed myself than any part of the machine.'

Just over a year after this crash, Albert Ball would become Britain's most successful ace of World War I. He would be called 'The English Richthofen', and his plane's red-painted propeller nose would strike fear into the hearts of enemy pilots.

❖   ❖   ❖

Born in Nottingham on 14 August 1896, Albert Ball was the son of a plumber who had become a successful local businessman and eventually Mayor of Nottingham. In 1911, young Albert was sent to Trent College. Life there was spartan – days started with getting up at 6.30, followed by a cold bath.

Ball was an average student, neither top nor bottom of his class. He wasn't particularly interested in sport, although he did join Nottingham Rowing Club. What really interested him was carpentry, photography, modelling and tinkering with old engines or pieces of electrical equipment. He loved working with his hands, solving practical problems, and would think nothing of spending a whole day taking a motor apart and putting it carefully back together again.

In his third and final year at Trent, Ball studied hard, intent on taking up a career in electrical engineering. He also joined the Officers Training Corps. Leaving college at seventeen, Ball started work at a small electrical company in Nottingham. He enjoyed his work but World War I was about to begin. On 4 August 1914, Britain officially declared war on Germany.

Within weeks, there were feverish recruiting drives all over Britain. 'Your Country Needs You' proclaimed posters of Lord Kitchener apparently pointing his finger straight at the viewer. Just a few weeks after his eighteenth birthday, Albert Ball answered the call and was enlisted as a private in the Nottingham and Derby Regiment.

That basic rank lasted only a few days. Once accommodation, uniforms, training and equipment had been sorted out for the thousands of new recruits, more appropriate ranks could be allocated. Within a week, Ball was promoted to sergeant mainly because of his time in the Officer Training Corps at Trent College.

During the winter of 1914/15 Ball went through his army training. He was desperate for the chance to do his duty. But, as 1915 drifted by, he seemed to be getting no nearer to the war in Europe; his unit was stationed in East London, where Britain feared Germany might attempt an invasion. As he already owned a motorbike, he asked to be transferred to an attachment of the Cyclist Division, thinking he might get to the front more quickly.

In June 1915, Ball was stationed not far from Hendon, where most of Britain's military pilots were trained. Suddenly he knew what he wanted to do. He paid for flying lessons out of his own pocket, hoping to join the newest branch of the British armed forces – the Royal Flying Corps (RFC).

Ball now began a tough regime, getting up at 3 a.m. most mornings. He raced over to Hendon on his motorbike and grabbed some instruction and flying time, before rushing back to be on parade by 6.45 a.m. The young man was frequently told off for the state of his uniform – covered in oil spluttered out by the aircraft's engines – but he was always back on time.

Learning to fly took far longer than Ball had imagined it would. Flights were constantly being cancelled due to the weather. It didn't just take storms and heavy rain to keep the training planes on the ground. Even a light wind, just above 15 kilometres per hour, was enough to prevent the frail craft taking to the air. Ball proved to be as average a pilot as he was a school student, but his enthusiasm carried him through a couple of crashes as well as seeing several other student pilots meet their deaths. In October, he received his basic pilot's licence and got a transfer to the RFC.

❖   ❖   ❖

February 1916 saw Ball finally get to France, having thirsted to take part in the war for eighteen months. He was attached to 13 squadron. But his job, flying a BE2c reconnaissance plane, quickly bored him. By the summer of 1916, he had pestered his commanding officers into having him trained as a fighter pilot. He performed so well in test flights that – young and inexperienced though he was – he was given the best fighter plane the Allies had at the time, the French Nieuport 16 Scout.

The French-made aircraft featured a single machine gun mounted on the top wing so it could fire straight ahead without sending shots through the propeller. Ball quickly got to grips with his new machine – in his first eleven combat flights he managed to force down at least five German aircraft. The number was probably higher, as he only ever claimed successes he was completely sure he had obtained by himself. His first complete victory came when he attacked and shot down a slow-moving two-seater German plane.

As Ball's confidence grew, he developed his trademark style of aerial combat, which relied less on strategy than on strong nerves. The airman began to make lone attacks on German planes flying in formation. His preferred tactic was to fly above, then swoop down below an enemy craft. Ball would wait until the very last second before firing his gun, tilting it upwards to shoot into the belly of the enemy machine. Absolutely fearless, he would attack, single out his man, and close in for the kill. On several occasions he almost rammed the enemy, while shot-down aircraft frequently missed his own plane by a whisker as they fell.

On the ground, he tended to keep himself to himself, growing plants on his home-made allotment on the airfield or tinkering with his aircraft or equipment. The skills Ball had developed during his time as an apprentice engineer didn't desert him. He spent much of his time on the ground checking his aircraft and making improvements which would give him an additional advantage over the enemy. For example, he readjusted his plane's controls so that for short periods he could fly no-handed, using both hands to aim his machine gun.

Ball was relentless. Whenever the weather cleared enough and his plane was repaired, he would be up in the air seeking another deadly combat. Any day in which an enemy plane wasn't shot down, damaged or forced to land was considered a 'dud day'. Ball had fewer of these than any other member of his squadron.

By the start of autumn 1916, Ball's tally had risen to an astonishing thirty official kills. But his success came at a price – he was on edge all the time. Worn out from the effort of battle, Britain's most successful flying ace was given leave to go back to Nottingham in October 1916.

❖　❖　❖

Ball looked forward to a rest and hoped to live a quiet life, maybe going fishing with his father and calming his shattered nerves. But he arrived home a national hero. Everyone wanted to see him and many functions were arranged in his honour. He even had breakfast with the Prime Minister, David Lloyd George.

Back in his home town, there was even more pomp and ceremony. The people of Nottingham had been grieving for three months over the loss of 500 men from a local battalion in a single day. They were desperate to celebrate the return of their famous war hero. Being naturally quiet and shy, Ball found all the attention hard to handle. Yet, wearily, he continued to be polite as he considered it part of his duty.

The authorities moved him to a post in Britain, helping to train student pilots. But Ball was too valuable an asset to be kept out of action for long. By February 1917, he was back in the thick of the fighting, assigned to 56 squadron.

❖ ❖ ❖

Ball left England for France with the newly formed 56 squadron, commanded by Major R.G. Blomfield. He was well-known as an efficient leader and strict on discipline, except where Albert Ball was concerned. Blomfield and Ball were often seen together, the Major in his spotless uniform and Ball with his boots covered in mud, shirt and tunic splattered in oil, and his unruly shock of black hair.

Ball had only been away from the front line for a few short months. Yet much had changed. The Germans had new aircraft and new tactics which were proving more successful. With more reliable machines and greater firepower on both sides, it was becoming vital to work as part of a disciplined team. To get separated and be singled out meant a quick end for British and German flyers alike.

Ball also had a new aircraft, the SE5A biplane fighter. The SE5A was, in many pilots' eyes, a vast improvement on previous fighters. It was strong, robust and fast. But, understandably, it took time for the quiet British ace to get used to it. He was allowed to keep his favourite aircraft, a Nieuport Scout, as a spare.

Although flying a different machine, Ball didn't see any need to change his tactics. On 23 April, he managed to shoot down three German aircraft – the squadron's very first kills. After this success, he continued to push himself hard. From dawn to dusk, he endeavoured to get into the air and attack as many German planes as possible. In the next fourteen days, he added a further fourteen kills to his tally – most attacked in his usual way, on his own and flying in dangerously close.

To many of his comrades, he seemed bulletproof. On one flight, even though all his controls were shot away, Ball managed to coax his plane down to a safe landing by winding his adjustable tailplane up and down. Having his plane shot up like this angered him so intensely that he wiped the engine oil off his hands and immediately ordered out his Nieuport fighter. He returned to the airfield within two hours, having downed another German aircraft.

On another flight, Ball was pounced upon by five German planes. He shot down two of them, before slamming his aircraft's control column forwards and letting his plane fall vertically towards the ground. He pulled the plane out of its fall just 10 metres from the earth's surface; one of the German fighters following him wasn't so lucky and crashed into the ground. Ball then attacked and shot down another, before finally returning to base.

At the end of April, in letters to his family, Ball wrote of how old and tired he felt. He had seen many good friends killed and he hoped the war would soon be over. He was offered two weeks' leave but insisted on staying in the front line. He now had forty-four kills to his name, though his fellow pilots reckoned that his real tally was many, many more.

❖   ❖   ❖

On 7 May 1917, Albert Ball took off with nine other aircraft from 56 squadron to lock horns with the enemy yet again. He was flying an SE5A two-winged biplane and they quickly engaged what appeared to be a group of German aircraft belonging to Baron von Richthofen's infamous Flying Circus. It was, in fact, led by the Red Baron's younger brother, Lothar von Richthofen. A furious series of dogfights commenced. It was chaos in the air, with first a German albatross fighter, painted red, bursting into flames, and then two shot-up SE5As leaving the battle to try and make forced landings.

One of 56 squadron's flyers, Captain Crowe, spotted Ball's aircraft in the distance. It dived and opened fire on a German plane below. Both Ball and the enemy he was chasing disappeared into heavy cloud. When the sky cleared, neither was to be seen.

Albert Ball didn't return to his squadron's airfield that day. Weeks later, photographs of his grave and a note were dropped over British lines by the Germans. The note read: 'R.F.C. Captain Ball was brought down in a fight in the air on the 7th of May, 1917, by a pilot who was of the same order as himself. He was buried at Annoeullin.'

❖   ❖   ❖

Albert Ball was awarded the Victoria Cross after his death, to go with his many other decorations including the Distinguished Service Order (DSO) and two bars – the equivalent of receiving the DSO three times.

Lothar Richthofen, brother of the famous Red Baron, was officially credited with bringing down Albert Ball's plane. But he claimed he had shot down a triplane before damage to his own craft had forced him to land. Ball's aircraft was a biplane.

The wreckage of Ball's SE5A was investigated at its crash site and only showed signs of crash damage, not the bullet holes and engine fire scars that mark a shot-down aircraft. Ball himself appeared to have died in the crash, with many broken bones but no bullet wounds. To this day, no one knows quite how Britain's most famous World War I ace lost his life.

◆　◆　◆

CHAPTER 2

A Natural Fighter

When World War I started, Britain still had an empire – a group of near and far-flung countries which it had helped colonize and, in many cases, still ruled. Known as the Commonwealth, these foreign states provided vital supplies, foodstuffs and large numbers of fighting men for the war. Commonwealth forces from Canada and the Indian subcontinent, for example, fought with great distinction.

Australia and New Zealand also provided thousands of men who all volunteered to fight for the Allied cause as members of the Australian and New Zealand Army Corps (known as the ANZACs). They remained the only solely volunteer force in World

War I, despite suffering terrible casualties. Among their best-remembered recruits was the first Commonwealth soldier to win a Victoria Cross, Albert Jacka.

◆ ◆ ◆

'Great battle at 3 a.m. Turks captured large portion of our trench. Lieut. Hamilton shot dead. I led a section of men and recaptured the trench.'

These words come from the diary of the Australian soldier, Albert Jacka. But the brief description scarcely does justice to the extraordinary feat which won him the Victoria Cross. Widely considered the finest Australian soldier of his day, Albert Jacka was always determined to do his best, to save his fellow allies, and to get through the war.

Albert was one of seven children, born at Winchelsea in the Australian state of Victoria. His father worked in the timber industry, and when Albert finished his schooling he worked for him for a while, before seeking a position in the Victoria State Forests Department at the age of eighteen.

Jacka was a good sportsman and loved cycling, boxing and playing Aussie Rules football. He won a number of cycle races in Northern Victoria and was a lively, tough character. Never slow to defend himself should a fight break out, he enlisted in the Australian Imperial Force (AIF) less than a month after World War I started. The 21-year-old's medical examination concluded that his health was sound but he was 'subject to teeth' – a polite way of saying that he was missing a few.

The call for Australians to join the war received a massive response. The authorities were overwhelmed by the number of volunteers and, somewhere in the mountain of paperwork, Albert Jacka's details went missing. He had to re-apply ten days later in Melbourne.

❖   ❖   ❖

The soldiers who formed the AIF were drawn from all classes and walks of life. Jacka was posted to 14th Battalion, which started its long sea journey to Europe on 22 December 1914. The battalion arrived in the Middle East and underwent two months of training before they embarked on the largest amphibious landing of the whole war – the Gallipoli campaign.

The aim of the Gallipoli campaign, embarked upon by ANZAC, British and French forces in late April 1915, was to invade an area of Turkey called the Dardanelles, of which the Gallipoli peninsula was a part. Once they had secured the peninsula, they hoped to progress to the city of Constantinople (now Istanbul), and knock Turkey, one of Germany's major allies, out of the war.

However these ambitions were not fulfilled, and the Gallipoli campaign is instead remembered as a dreadful military tragedy, where the incredible resolve, skill and bravery of thousands of soldiers was undermined by bad planning on the part of High Command. Strategy was bungled, successful attacks were not followed up, and the generals underestimated the strength and resolve of the Turkish forces. By the early part of 1916, when the campaign was finally dissolved by the Allies, over 200,000 men had lost their lives. The only success was the mass evacuation of ANZAC and British troops from the area – an operation which resulted in no casualties.

❖   ❖   ❖

Battle lines in World War I were frequently drawn very close. During the Gallipoli campaign, the enemy forces were sometimes so near each other that home-made bombs and grenades could be lobbed by hand into the opposing trenches. Courtney's Post was one such terrifying place. It was here that Albert Jacka won his VC, less than a month after the ANZAC forces landed.

On 19 May, the Turks launched a major attack, aiming to drive the Allies out of their precarious footholds on the shoreline and into the sea. The fighting was ferocious and there were casualties on both sides. The Turks secured a stretch of the trenches at Courtney's Post but Australian forces fought to the death to prevent them invading further. Jacka was caught in one part of the trench, single-handedly fighting off the Turks nearby. An officer, Lieutenant Hamilton, tried to join him to help, but was quickly shot dead. Another officer, Lieutenant Crabbe, raced to the area. Jacka was isolated and fighting for his life, but nevertheless he shouted and gestured to Crabbe not to join him, for he would have taken the same lethal path as Hamilton.

Jacka eventually broke free, but not before dragging a wounded man to safety. He then approached Lieutenant Crabbe with a plan for re-taking the trench area. This called for massed troops to create a diversion at one end of the captured section of trench while Albert attacked all by himself from the other. Under cover of darkness, Jacka crept round behind the Turks and waited for the diversion to begin.

The other troops opened up with their rifles and threw two bombs into the trench. Meanwhile, Jacka leaped into the trench and started firing. He shot five Turkish soldiers and used the bayonet on the end of his rifle to attack two more. The remaining enemy troops fled from the trench but Jacka stayed, guarding the area calmly until he was reunited with his fellow members of 14th Battalion. Legend has it that when Lieutenant Crabbe found him he was sitting in the trench full of dead bodies, with an unlit cigarette in his mouth, and remarked, 'Well, I got the beggars, sir.'

Jacka was awarded the VC for his exploits, but his action at Courtney's Point, Gallipoli, proved to be just one of many incredible feats of courage during his active war service.

❖ ❖ ❖

After the retreat at Gallipoli, many of the AIF troops were re-deployed on the Western Front, Jacka among them. He continued to lead from the front, inspiring his comrades. The action at Pozières, in August 1916, ranked among the most dramatic of the entire war.

The 7th German Infantry had advanced at the crack of dawn. They stormed through the forward positions of the Australian troops, took many prisoners and looked to be breaking through the lines. Jacka, now a lieutenant, was in a dugout, resting with some of his men, when the Germans overran them. It looked as if Jacka and his remaining men would be taken prisoner but Albert was having none of it.

In the chaos that followed, he shot the first German sent to their dugout to guard them, and then led eight men out of the trenches to a position above ground. As always, he took the lead, inspiring other troops to follow him in attacking the German forces who, having advanced so far, were now being hit from behind.

Jacka was hit three times as he approached an enemy position created by a heavy artillery shell. In his own words, each bullet 'swung me off my feet. But each time I sprung up like a prizefighter, and kept getting closer.'

Despite being badly wounded, he still managed to leap into the shellhole and to battle and vanquish the four Germans inside. His example was followed by others and a potential break in the Allied lines was prevented, with many Germans taken prisoner. Seriously injured and transported away from the front line for treatment, Jacka received the Military Cross, a significant decoration but a lower-ranked medal than the Victoria Cross.

Once he had recovered from his wounds, Jacka carried out a risky, lone reconnaisance mission at a place called Messines, before leading a company of soldiers to capture 800 metres of enemy-held ground. At Bullecourt, in April 1917, he made a dangerous move through the wire of the enemy fortifications (known as the Hindenburg Line). He was on his own when two German soldiers approached. His gun failed to fire but Jacka rushed them and after a struggle brought them back to the Australian lines as prisoners.

❖   ❖   ❖

For this last action, Jacka received another bar to the Military Cross he won at Pozières. Many military historians believe that Jacka deserved additional Victoria Crosses for both his actions at Bullecourt and, especially, Pozières. Jacka, himself, although modest about his bravery and achievements in general, also believed that these feats were more daring than his first, at Gallipoli.

But, despite his abilities, actions and experience, Jacka was never awarded another VC and he never rose above the rank of captain. There are many possible reasons for this. During World War I, there was usually a very marked dividing line between the officers and the 'ranks' (the soldiers commanded by the officers). Jacka didn't like this divide. As a result of his down-to-earth approach to leadership and his vast experience, he was extremely popular with his men, who trusted and admired him.

However, some of his immediate superior officers, frequently with far less battlefield experience, felt intimidated by a man who had seen and done it all. Jacka had already received the highest possible award, and his outspoken nature did not endear himself to the majors and colonels he came in contact with. He was not one for playing politics and trying to impress senior officers. He was more concerned with the welfare of his fellow servicemen and the ultimate goal of winning the war.

By the time Jacka recovered from a wound he received in July 1917 and was back with his battalion, he was virtually in charge, despite his relatively low rank. The soldiers all revered 'Bert Jacka' – their incredible Captain who led from the front whenever the chance arose. The battalion became known as 'Jacka's Mob'.

In May 1918 Jacka suffered badly from a German attack using poison gas. He was also wounded for the second time in the throat. Many feared that he would not survive. He was evacuated to Britain where he underwent several life-and-death operations. Jacka did survive, but had to go through a very long period of recovery. Over a year passed before he returned to Australia. He was one of the last Australian servicemen to head home, long after the Armistice had been signed and World War I had ended.

❖   ❖   ❖

In Melbourne, Albert received a massive hero's welcome. With little formal education and no great career prospects, it would have been understandable if he had traded on his fame and incredible popularity to earn an easy life. For example, he was offered the job of Victorian Police Commissioner, on a handsome salary, in 1920. But he declined the offer. Instead, Jacka formed an import business with another officer he knew from 14th Battalion, E.T. Edmonds.

For a time, the business went well and Jacka became a popular councillor in an area of Melbourne called St Kilda. But the Great Depression hit Australia very hard in 1930, and the business collapsed when the owner of most of the company's shares sold them at a large loss. At around the same time, Jacka found himself elected as Mayor of St Kilda. He continued to do what he had done as a councillor – fight hard for the welfare of ordinary people, especially the unemployed – despite his own troubles.

The following year, Jacka was worn out and did not stand for re-election as mayor. He was offered yet more chances to trade on his fame but refused, instead finding employment as a travelling sales-man. But his health quickly failed and he was admitted to hospital in December 1931. He died less than a month later.

The public came out in droves to see Jacka buried with full military honours at St Kilda Cemetery. Eight former military men acted as pallbearers and carried Jacka's coffin at his funeral.

All eight were also Victoria Cross winners – a fitting tribute to one of the most daring and accomplished infantrymen of the entire war. But perhaps the best tribute of all came from Jacka's own lips. His final words, uttered to his father, were, 'I'm still fighting, Dad.'

◆ ◆ ◆

CHAPTER 3

Devotion to Duty

At the start of World War I, many Allied soldiers were left trapped behind enemy lines after a battle at Mons in Belgium. Most were taken prisoner by the Germans, but some avoided capture. They needed much help to get back to safety. Many people risked their own lives in order to shelter and assist these fugitives. One of this number was an English nurse called Edith Cavell.

◆ ◆ ◆

It was a cold, wet night in November 1914 when a knock was heard at the door of the nurses' school in Brussels, the Belgian capital. Two escaped

British soldiers, Sergeant Meachin and Colonel Bolger, one badly wounded, the other only slightly injured, had been guided through the streets by a Belgian engineer. They had evaded capture for many weeks but time was running out. If they were caught by the German forces occupying Belgium, both the soldiers and their guide faced imprisonment or death.

The front door of the nurses' school opened, and they were escorted inside. There they met a woman who was aware of the dangers but could not refuse to treat people in need. Her name was Edith Cavell and her devotion to duty was so strong that she succeeded in helping over 200 British, French and Belgian troops escape the Germans' clutches.

❖   ❖   ❖

Edith Cavell was born in the village of Swardeston, near Norwich, in 1865, the daughter of the local vicar. The family were far from wealthy but were highly religious and considered caring for others to be the most important part of life. Before their evening meal, they often carried a portion of meat to poorer families in the village. There was fun to be had, sketching the country scenes, playing in the fields and gardens around their home in summer, and skating and tobogganing in the winter. But self-sacrifice, simple living and prayer were key elements in the upbringing of Edith, her two sisters and one brother.

Edith was the most serious of the four Cavell children and showed a talent for learning foreign languages, especially French. She became a governess to a family in Brussels in the 1890s and stayed there until she had to return home to help care for her ill father. Hitting upon the vocation that most suited her, she studied to become a nurse and worked in a hospital at Tooting in South London and then in the East End of London – at the time, a place of desperate poverty.

In 1907 she accepted a prestigious appointment. She became Matron of Belgium's first training school for nurses. By now, Edith Cavell had grown up into a strict, serious woman who kept herself to herself and had never married. She was a hard taskmaster but she was also honest, fair and very professional, highly respected by her staff, colleagues and students.

❖   ❖   ❖

In Belgium, unlike England, there was no proper training for nurses. Many nurses there were nuns, with little or no medical education. Cavell worked tirelessly to build up the nursing school, in the centre of Brussels, to treat the poor and the needy and to produce good nurses. It was such a success that a new, purpose-built centre was being constructed when World War I started.

By late August 1914, German forces had captured Brussels with little fighting. After the Germans attacked and ruined the Belgian city of Louvain, the Belgian king, Albert I, ordered his forces not to resist. Cavell could have returned to Britain and safety but she refused. Instead, she insisted on staying with her nurses, treating all who needed care, no matter which side they were on. For a short time, before the German advance swept on past Brussels, there was a strange mixture of German soldiers and local Belgians being cared for at the nursing centre.

If Cavell had simply performed her nursing duty in the middle of a war-torn country during World War I, her story would have been interesting. The fact that she was a British woman working in a part of Europe occupied by the enemy made it more so. But it became truly remarkable with the events of late 1914.

The night of the 1 November 1914 changed everything. It was the moment when the first two fugitive British soldiers appeared at the nursing school. Sergeant Meachin had a grazed head but his superior, Colonel Bolger, had a serious leg wound as well as other injuries. Both had been on the run for many weeks and needed help.

Bolger and Meachin had been caught by the Germans and taken to a temporary hospital but had escaped. They needed treatment and shelter. Cavell could have refused them help but she kept quiet and did not betray them. She chose to assist them at her own risk. They stayed at her nursing school for two weeks. At one point, there was a narrow escape when Cavell received news that the Germans were going to search the buildings. Luckily, she was able to have the two soldiers escorted to a nearby house just in time. Finally, she arranged to lead the two men out of the immediate area.

❖ ❖ ❖

News of Cavell's success quickly reached a Belgian aristocrat, Prince Reginald de Croy, who was leading an underground organization which escorted Allied soldiers back to safety. He asked her to join their efforts. Their objective was to scour the region for fugitive Allied troops whom they then hid, provided with food, money, and civilian clothes, and relocated to avoid capture by the Germans. Despite the risks, Cavell agreed to help.

Her part in the operation was crucial and highly dangerous. She was to provide an important refuge for the men at her nursing home, as a stepping stone to their eventual escape over the border with

Holland and into Allied territory. As it turned out, Cavell offered a lot more. She arranged money, guides and identification papers for the fugitive soldiers. The papers were forged by other members of the group and Cavell took many of the passport photographs, using an old Box Brownie camera. On more than one occasion, she even had to act as a guide herself, collecting fugitive French and British soldiers at crowded tramways and train stations.

The danger of being found out increased every day, along with the tension and stress. Cavell still had a busy nursing school to run but did almost all the dangerous work with the fugitive soldiers herself. This was mainly so that as few people as possible would be in trouble should the Germans realize what was going on. The German authorities had issued an order stating that anyone found to be sheltering Allied troops would be shot. Edith wrote to her cousin, 'I am helping in ways I may not describe to you till we are free.'

Despite strict food rationing, Cavell somehow managed to feed not only her staff and the real patients but also the hidden escapees. They were placed in unoccupied beds in the nursing school, pretending to be patients, or hidden in the cellars of the building. Much of the time, Cavell cooked food for them herself at night. She would serve them and wash all the dishes up late in the evening so that no trace was left.

❖   ❖   ❖

The underground organization of which Cavell was now a member worked well and helped many British, French and Belgian soldiers escape. It also assisted young French and Belgian men to leave regions occupied by the Germans so that they could enlist and train as soldiers for the Allies.

The trickle of fugitives became a flood. At one desperate point, Cavell was sheltering thirty-five escapees. In her heart of hearts, she knew that the Germans were sure to find out, but it didn't stop her doing everything she could to assist the escaping men.

Few of those who came through the nursing school ever forgot the devotion and courage of its head. The fact that there was not more acclaim for Cavell was due to her charges keeping quiet while she was still alive and aiding other soldiers. She even gave one fugitive, Corporal Sheldrake, one of her own shirts to wear as a disguise. He was so touched by her aid that when he died he left instructions that he wished to be buried in that garment.

❖   ❖   ❖

As more and more Allied soldiers were successfully harboured, rumours gradually grew of Cavell's work. The German authorities were suspicious but could not be sure. They started to keep the nursing home under careful watch. There were many narrow escapes. Once, a soldier had to hide in a barrel of apples to avoid detection. Visits from the German secret police became more frequent, and several patients who Cavell trusted and took in were, without doubt, informers for the Germans.

By the middle of 1915, Edith Cavell had lodged more than 100 British and an additional 100 French and Belgian soldiers. Comings and goings at the Institute had become so frequent that the Germans were close to pouncing. It was obvious that the escape route could not be kept open for much longer. Collegues urged her to escape while she could, but she refused. In letters to people she trusted, Cavell gave the impression that she knew it was only a matter of time before the Germans discovered what she was doing and arrested her.

The head of the escape organization, Prince de Croy, visited Brussels to warn her of the impending danger. He called on Cavell in her office and told her he was going into hiding and that she should flee, too.

'I expect to be arrested. Escape for me is futile and unthinkable,' she replied.

Argue as he might, Prince de Croy knew he was facing a person whose mind he could not change. He left and escaped over the border into Allied territory.

❖   ❖   ❖

Cavell was right to expect a call from the Germans. At the end of July, a key member of the escape organization, Philippe Baucq, was arrested and his house searched. He had destroyed much evidence that could lead the Germans to others, but unfortunately he hadn't burned two letters which contained information about Edith Cavell.

On 5 August 1915, Otto Mayer turned up at Cavell's nursing school. He was a high-ranking German secret policeman and questioned her back at his headquarters while the nursing centre was thoroughly searched. Due to careful planning by Cavell and others, nothing of importance was found. Edith's diary remained where she had hidden it, sewn into a chair cushion. It remained there undiscovered for thirty years and is now in the Imperial War Museum in London.

There is, to this day, confusion over precisely how much Edith Cavell told the Germans. Some believe she didn't say anything more than the Germans had already learned. Others state that she was tricked by the German Secret Police into believing that they already knew of all those involved and that she gave up important details. Certainly, the Germans did their best to give the impression that Cavell had betrayed all her friends, an action which seems at odds with her character.

❖ ❖ ❖

On 7 October, Cavell and thirty-four other prisoners – guides, escape organizers and people who had provided shelter or assistance – were committed to trial. They were brought before a German military court and their lawyers were given no time to arrange their defence. The trial ended with prison sentences for most of the accused. Cavell, Philippe Baucq and three others fared worse. They were sentenced to death.

The Germans tried to keep the trial and its results secret but word quickly leaked out. Government officials from Spain and the United States both visited the German authorities, begging that the death sentences be changed to imprisonment. The military governor, new to the region and wishing to show his toughness, would not change the court's decision. It had been decided that Cavell and Baucq were to be executed as soon as possible.

Cavell was informed of her impending fate and took the news calmly. Her strength of purpose stayed with her to the very end. The German prison guards were touched by her calm manner and her genuine concern for their welfare.

Cavell's last words have become famous in themselves. Her last British visitor was a man called Stirling Gahan. He was the English chaplain in Brussels. They prayed together, spoke the hymn, 'Abide with Me' and talked a little.

'I have no fear,' she said. 'I have seen death so often it is not strange to me.' Gahan reported her last words as, 'Standing as I do, in view of God and eternity, I realize that patriotism is not enough: I must have no hatred or bitterness towards anyone.'

Cavell was taken to the National Rifle Range at Brussels. There, on 12 October 1915, she and Philippe Baucq were tied to posts and had their eyes covered. At dawn, a firing squad opened fire. Edith Cavell was forty-nine years old and still wearing her nurse's uniform when she was shot.

❖   ❖   ❖

The Germans had made a terrible propaganda mistake. Edith Cavell's fate provoked outrage all over the world. In Britain and other countries, images of her were used to encourage recruitment to the armed forces to fight the 'murdering monsters' of Germany. Allied recruitment doubled for eight weeks after her death was announced.

Originally, her body was buried where it had fallen at the rifle range in Brussels. But in 1919 she was brought back to England and reburied in Norwich Cathedral. The authorities had offered the heroine's family the chance to bury her at Westminster Abbey, but her parents believed she would have preferred to have been laid to rest closer to her family home of Swardeston.

Memorials to Cavell exist at her local Swardeston church, at Norwich Cathedral, in the centre of London, and in other countries of the world. They exist to commemorate this shy, stubborn and incredibly brave nurse who ceaselessly did her duty with no thought of her own safety.

◆ ◆ ◆

CHAPTER 4

Lawrence of Arabia

When World War I started, much of what we now call the Middle East was under the control of foreign powers, particularly the Turkish Ottoman Empire which ran states such as Syria, Lebanon, Israel (then known as Palestine) and Jordan. Military operations in the Middle East were beset with problems. Apart from the incredible heat, the desert conditions and the long distances between waterholes and settlements, there was a huge gulf between Arab and European cultures.

The Arabs were no friends of Turkey, nor its major ally Germany, and they wanted independence. Yet the Allied forces had no understanding of Arab ways and customs. As a result, early attempts at mobilizing them to fight against the Turks and the Germans came to nothing. It took the will and personality of one man with a real passion for the Arab peoples to gain their trust and play an important part in focusing the Arab uprising.

❖ ❖ ❖

Clad in Arab robes, Lieutenant Thomas Edward Lawrence strode into Allied command headquarters in Cairo to general astonishment. Military police attempted to arrest and interrogate this Arab with his silk robes, gold head rope and dagger, but he spoke perfect English and insisted that they send reinforcements and supplies to support the Arab forces which had just taken Aqaba.

The British personnel were amazed. Aqaba was a prize they had hoped for but had not quite known how to obtain. Lawrence was interviewed by several senior officers but it didn't take long for him to convince them, and a supply ship was despatched at great speed. It was July 1917 and Lawrence had just taken part in one of the most epic missions of the entire war.

❖ ❖ ❖

Born in 1888, Lawrence was fascinated by archaeology from a young age and studied the subject at Oxford University. In order to complete a project on the castles of the Crusades, the young T.E. Lawrence made a hazardous lone journey. During the summer of 1909, he walked through large parts of Syria living as an Arab and studying the sites and the peoples. On one occasion he was beaten by a band of tribespeople and left for dead, yet Lawrence returned to Britain with a deep regard for Arab customs and traditions.

Shortly after war broke out, Lawrence spent a brief period in London working for the government department known as the War Office on maps and other geographical information. He was then posted to the Military Intelligence Department in Cairo – the capital city of Egypt – where he met many Arab nationalist leaders who wanted independence from the Turkish Empire. Lawrence was more successful than most Allied diplomats and soldiers in forging links with the heads of the Arab tribes. His word quickly became trusted, particularly by an important Arab leader called Emir Feisal.

In 1916, Lawrence was appointed as a direct military adviser to Feisal as he started to organize the many small Arab tribes into a fighting force united against the Turks. Feisal was an enormously patient, intelligent and impressive leader, from whom Lawrence learned a great deal.

By now, Lawrence dressed like an Arab in

flowing robes which kept the glaring sun at bay. He had learned not only to ride a camel, but to ride one at top speed. He ate the same food as his Arab hosts and generally followed the same customs as them. Through this respect for the Arab way of life and his sheer force of personality, he became highly valued by many of the Arab leaders.

❖　❖　❖

Early Arab actions, mainly against important railway supply lines, were largely successful. Lawrence had been fully involved in many of these attacks, surviving by the skin of his teeth on several occasions. He soon developed something of a gift for handling and setting off explosives to damage train lines. But by the spring of 1917, exhaustion, dysentery and fever forced Lawrence to rest for ten days. Nevertheless, his mind stayed active and he planned the attack on the Syrian port of Aqaba.

Although the campaigns in late 1916 and early 1917, in an area of the Middle East known as Hedjaz (now part of Saudia Arabia), had been successful, it was difficult for the Arab nationalists to advance further north without any means of getting support and supplies. Aqaba, a port at the northern end of the Red Sea, would make the perfect supply point but it was controlled by the Turks.

Lawrence had visited Aqaba before the war, and he knew from his intelligence work in Cairo that the Turks had built heavy defences in the narrow pass connecting the town to its major waterhole, the Wadi Itm. He realized that capturing Aqaba without the water supply would be pointless, so he came up with a daring and dangerous plan which the Arab forces agreed with.

❖ ❖ ❖

On 9 May 1917, Lawrence, Auda (a leader of the Abu Tayi tribe) and some forty or so others set off on a long trek. They were led by an important follower of Emir Feisal, a man called Nasir. Their long, looping route through the harsh desert covered almost 800 kilometres, and their eventual aim was to reach and attack Wadi Itm from behind. Each man rode a camel equipped with a rifle, spare ammunition, over 20 kilograms of flour (with which to make bread), and water.

The first couple of days took them over relatively easy ground but soon they reached the difficult desert tracks where they lost two of their camels. In less than a week, Lawrence was again beset by fever and also by raging boils across his back. He feared for the camel train and worried that he was helping to lead men he admired to certain death. But he kept these fears to himself and continued onwards.

The trek wasn't just over endless sand dunes. Sometimes the camel train had to cross solid lava plains. Once they had to cross beds of sharp flints which cut the camels' feet. And there were plenty of other threats. Treacherous sandstorms repeatedly swept the desert; in the blinding swirl of dust, there was a danger of becoming separated from the group. There was also the possibility of attack – both from rogue groups of Turkish soldiers and from other, hostile, Arab groups. On one occasion, the camel train was fired upon by another Arab tribe, but fortunately they retreated before a full-scale battle could take place.

On 21 May, skin cracked and blackened from the sun, Lawrence and the Arabs reached an area of fertile land. Here, they found a well which replenished their water supplies. And several of the Arabs managed to track down and kill two gazelles, providing the camel train with much-needed nourishment. Like the Arabs he was with, Lawrence was used to eating only every other day and going for long periods without water. But on this day the forty-strong camel train sat down to a desert feast of meat, bread, water and Arabic coffee. Stomachs were filled and spirits were raised.

However, the next few days were even tougher than before. More camels died of exhaustion or illness and progress was slow. Against the wishes of the Arab leaders, Nasir and Auda, Lawrence tracked back to rescue a man called Gasim, who had fallen behind and lost his way. Without the Briton's intervention, he would have perished. By 27 May, the trek through the hostile, empty desert was over. The party had reached the camping grounds of a friendly tribe – the Howeitat – who treated them extremely well, with feasts and entertainment.

❖   ❖   ❖

Lawrence was relieved but he knew they had achieved nothing yet. They were deep inside Turkish-held territory and they had to spread word of their plan quickly among other groups of Arabs in order to boost their measly force of forty into the hundreds necessary for an attack. The next few weeks saw Auda, Nasir and Lawrence all ride off on short, separate missions to drum up support.

On 19 June, over 500 men on camels set out for Aqaba. Meanwhile, Lawrence had taken a fifth of the force over 180 kilometres further north to cause a diversion by attacking the Turkish-controlled railway at a place called Deraa. His explosives expertise was again put to good use. The mission was successful and the group rejoined the main force, tired, but without a single casualty.

Many of the waterholes and wells on their route

to Aqaba had been destroyed or blocked by the Turks but Lawrence and others managed to open one to supply their force. A small Turkish fortification, called a blockhouse, was attacked and overcome by the Arabs with ease. Soon after, they damaged yet another stretch of railway line. By now, Lawrence had earned the Arabic name El Orens ('destroyer of railroads').

❖ ❖ ❖

The force travelled closer to Aqaba until their way was blocked at Aba el Lissan. The blockhouse there proved a far tougher proposition. It had been reinforced with many Turkish soldiers and the first attempts at attack were not successful. Small raiding groups were sent to aim sniper fire at the Turks and to creep behind their lines and cut telephone and telegraph wires, but many of the Arabs were getting impatient.

Auda and Lawrence had an argument over the lack of action and Auda set off with fifty horsemen to charge the Turks at the blockhouse. Lawrence leaped on to his camel and joined Auda and his men. Charging towards the Turkish positions, the Englishman found himself riding ahead of the horsemen. Suddenly, he was right in the middle of the surprised Turks. Firing shots from his revolver this way and that, Lawrence then found his camel giving way beneath him. The camel had been shot dead, and both it and the British soldier hit the ground hard.

Lawrence lay prone on the ground as the rest of the Arab force, led by Nasir, mounted a 400-strong camel charge which threatened to trample him to death. Huddling next to the dead camel, Lawrence survived as the charge flowed around him. The Arabs fought fiercely and the Turks were no match for them. Aba el Lissan had fallen and with it many Turkish soldiers. Around 120 were taken prisoner, while the Arabs had lost only a handful of fighters.

Excited by their success, the Arabs desperately wanted to press on and attack a big Turkish garrison at Maan. It took all Lawrence's powers of persuasion to convince them to continue on to their key target, Aqaba. Turkish resistance after this point was limited. The Arabs secured the Wadi Itm and the news spread among the Arab peoples near Aqaba. The forces grew and grew in number. Lawrence sent a message to the Turks inside Aqaba that if they did not give up at once, he could not answer for the actions of the Arabs he was with. The Turks immediately waved a white flag in response.

Lawrence's important role in the capture of Aqaba was recognized by his commanders locally. He received medals from both Britain and France –

not that he was particularly interested in decorations such as these. He stayed with the Arab forces and became the chief link between the head of the Allied forces in the Middle East and the Arab armies led by Feisal. The Arab revolt increased in scale and pace and Lawrence continued to play a full part in it, both as an active soldier and as an organizer.

❖ ❖ ❖

Lawrence's life continued to be eventful after World War I, when he lobbied tirelessly for Arab independence from colonial rule. He attended the 1919 Paris Peace Conference but could not stop three of the Arab states, Syria, Palestine and Mesopotamia (now Iraq) coming under French and British control.

He started to become famous as a result of various lectures and books about his escapades, especially those produced by a British poet, Robert Graves, and an American journalist, Lowell Thomas, who gave dozens of sold-out lectures about 'Lawrence of Arabia'. For several years, Lawrence traded on his fame in order to press the case for Arab independence.

Then, in 1921, with British control of Mesopotamia threatened by rebellion, the politician Winston Churchill was appointed to search for a solution. Churchill convinced Lawrence to join him as an adviser and the end result was that Lawrence's old friend, Emir Feisal, was appointed as the rebellious country's leader. Much more self-rule was allowed, although the country remained a British colony.

Exhausted from his diplomatic efforts and the pressure of his increasing fame, Lawrence used fake names and contacts in the military to join the Royal Air Force (RAF), and then, when the newspapers discovered this ruse, to enlist in the Tank Corps. He rejoined the RAF in the mid-1920s and went on to play an important part in developing high-speed boats, known as crashboats, used to recover downed pilots and aircrew.

Throughout this time, Lawrence wrote, rewrote and revised what he hoped would be his masterpiece, a book which he eventually published under the title Seven Pillars of Wisdom. It became a huge bestseller and helped fuel the legend of Lawrence of Arabia. He retired from the military in 1935, hoping to devote his time to more writing and publishing projects, but less than two months later, while out on his motorbike, he was involved in an accident. He swerved to avoid two boys on bicycles, was thrown from his motorbike and died six days later from the serious head injuries he suffered.

❖ ❖ ❖

The life and achievements of T. E. Lawrence are cloaked in myth and speculation. Certainly, Lawrence himself was prone to exaggeration and did little to stop others trumpeting his achievements. But what does seem clear from witnesses, from military records, and from the thousands of pages of books and research on his life, is that T. E. Lawrence was an extraordinary individual.

Rarely do major events in a war hinge on the actions of one soldier of relatively low rank, but it is fair to say that Lawrence made an incredible difference. Through his understanding and deep regard for the Arabs and their ways, he was able to help forge the Arab tribespeople into an effective and successful fighting unit, and thus help to change the course of the war in the Middle East.

◆ ◆ ◆

CHAPTER 5

The Courageous Doctor Chavasse

The casualties in World War I were horrendous. Over ten million active servicemen were killed, double that number were wounded, and many millions of civilians died as an indirect result of the conflict. Servicemen and some women died from bullet wounds or explosions from landmines, from mortar fire or from heavy artillery weapons. The awful conditions in the trenches, where soldiers suffered intense cold, constant flooding and raging disease, accounted for hundreds of thousands more casualties.

Yet the losses would have been even higher had it not been for the efforts of the medical units attached to the armies of both sides. Far from staying in safety behind the lines, many doctors, nurses, orderlies and stretcher-bearers constantly risked their own lives in order to help the injured. Noel Godfrey Chavasse was one such doctor, whose bravery and devotion to duty inspired many around him.

◆　◆　◆

In November 1884, two identical male twins were born to Edith Chavasse and her husband, the Reverend Francis James Chavasse. They were named Christopher and Noel, with Christopher being the eldest by just twenty minutes. The twins had two other brothers, Bernard and Aidan, and three sisters, Edith, Mary and Dorothea. When Noel and Christopher were just five, the family moved from Oxford to Liverpool where their father became Bishop and the children went to school at Liverpool College. At the age of twenty, Christopher and Noel both went back to Oxford and enrolled at the university, Christopher to study history, and his brother, natural sciences. Noel planned to become a doctor and eventually perform missionary work.

In 1907, Noel graduated with First Class Honours but Christopher failed and this led him to have a nervous breakdown. However, he pulled through and re-sat his exams. Both twins were keen athletes and played many different sports, including lacrosse, rugby and athletics. In fact, to their family's delight, they were both chosen to represent Great Britain at the 1908 Olympics. Both ran in the 400 metres, then known as the 440 yards flat or quarter mile.

In January 1909, Noel joined the Oxford University Officer Training Corps Medical Unit, and in July of the same year completed his studies at Oxford. Christopher was studying to enter the Church and this was the time when their paths started to diverge. Noel enrolled to study medicine, and by mid-July 1912 he had passed his final medical exams and was a fully qualified doctor. His first placement was at the Royal Southern Hospital in Liverpool. It was hard work with very long hours but Chavasse enjoyed helping others and making a positive difference.

He became a member of the Royal Army Medical Corps (RAMC) in 1913 and was assigned to the 10th Battalion of the Kings (Liverpool Regiment), better known as the Liverpool Scottish. He still had his duties at the hospital, as well as serving in the part-time reserve force known as the Territorial Army. These years, 1913 and 1914, were hectic for the 29-year-old doctor.

❖   ❖   ❖

On 1 November 1914, Noel and the rest of the Liverpool Scottish boarded a ship at Southampton Docks. They were on their way to France. His twin was already there, as chaplain to a hospital unit based at St Nazaire. All four Chavasse brothers would soon see active service in Europe. Noel's army unit was just one of many which had been fully mobilized in the war against Germany and her allies (Turkey, the Austro-Hungarian Empire and Bulgaria), together known as the Central Powers.

❖   ❖   ❖

Near the end of the same month, the Liverpool Scottish reached the front line. Within twenty-four hours of their arrival, Noel's good friend Captain Arthur Twentyman became the first member of the Liverpool Scottish to die. He was far from the last.

Chavasse was operating behind the front line but was by no means safe from enemy attack. Many times he had to sprint through enemy shelling and sniper fire to attend a hit comrade. He fought hard to save the most seriously wounded men and also to prevent less seriously injured soldiers catching diseases and other ailments and dying as a result.

The conditions in the trenches are hard for people today to imagine. Dug into the ground and reinforced, in places, by wooden supports, with planks (called duckboards) to walk on, the trenches became rivers of mud after heavy rain. Soldiers had to live, fight, eat, sleep, wash and, sometimes, even relieve themselves in a narrow trench which was open to the elements.

These were ideal conditions for lice, exposure and a host of diseases. As the war progressed, conditions got worse and worse. After an attack, the bodies of the dead were often buried in the repaired trench wall. Outdoor toilets, hit by shelling, would spill filth everywhere. Not surprisingly, soldiers reported large numbers of rats, some almost as big as cats, swarming around.

Chavasse, like other medics, struggled to treat men in these squalid, unhygienic conditions. By the time he had cut through a patient's muddy uniform, he would be as filthy as the soldier he was caring for. And winter in the trenches brought additional hazards. Soldiers were often forbidden to light fires in case the enemy spotted the smoke, so frostbite, influenza viruses and illness due to the severe cold caused many deaths.

❖   ❖   ❖

In March 1915, the battalion was sent to Ypres, in Belgium, in time for a major offensive the following month. The Second Battle of Ypres was the first to feature poisonous chlorine gas used as a weapon. Chavasse's unit did not directly experience the

German gas attacks, but they were greatly upset by rumours that it destroyed the lungs and caused a slow, painful death by suffocation.

In June, the battalion was involved in the Battle of Hooge. And Chavasse was eventually awarded a Military Cross for risking his own life to save others, having regularly scoured dangerous, shell-torn areas for wounded soldiers to treat. But it was little comfort to the doctor, who had lost many good friends. In just over six months, the battalion had been reduced from more than 850 fit officers and men to fewer than 150. Reinforcements were sent out and the Liverpool Scottish continued its active service.

❖   ❖   ❖

A year after the Battle of Hooge saw the start of one of the biggest and most costly campaigns of World War I – the Somme. Noel Chavasse, now promoted to Captain and still with the Liverpool Scottish, accompanied his unit to the Somme as they were ordered to attack a place called Guillemont in July of that year. The attack didn't go well from the start. Instructions as to which route to take were unclear and there was much confusion. Heavy machine-gun fire from the German positions swept the advancing forces.

Chavasse tended the wounded throughout the

action, without even the little bit of cover and protection offered by a trench. Four times the forces tried to advance and each time they were pinned back. The Liverpool Scottish lost seventy-four men killed, a number missing, and over 170 wounded, but the numbers would have been far higher had it not been for the bravery of Chavasse and others.

Again and again, the medic ventured forward to rescue wounded men as well as treating those who made it back to his aid post. At one point he was wounded in the side by a shell fragment, but still helped to carry back an urgent case for half a kilometre.

When night fell, Chavasse and several volunteers ventured into the potentially lethal area between the two sides' positions known as No Man's Land. There they crept around, dodging shells and gunfire to retrieve seriously wounded soldiers. For four hours, the brave doctor repeatedly swept No Man's Land looking for patients to treat. At one point, Chavasse and the others were less than 25 metres away from the German front line when they found three wounded soldiers sheltering in a shellhole.

The small group of volunteers led by Chavasse saved around twenty men who normally wouldn't have had a chance of survival, and this action eventually won him the Victoria Cross. He was granted a period of sick leave to recover from his wounds but rejoined the battalion by early September.

Immediately, they were back in action at a place called Delville Wood. 'Shortly after, Noel was reprimanded for criticizing some of the actions of his superiors and was placed well behind enemy lines to work in a hospital. But by Christmas 1916, he was back in the front line, risking all to save his fellow soldiers' lives.

❖ ❖ ❖

Some respite came in February 1917, when Noel was given two weeks' leave. One of his first duties on returning to England was to travel to Buckingham Palace. There, he received his Victoria Cross. During this period of leave, he also spent some time with his long-time love, Gladys. (The couple had already agreed to marry at a future date, when Chavasse returned and the war was over.) Then, returning to the same battalion, he continued his tireless work in increasingly hostile conditions.

Tragedy struck the Chavasse family on the first day of July. Just a few kilometres from where Noel's unit was stationed, his brother, Aidan, went out on a raiding party and was seen to be wounded. He never returned and his is just one of a horrific 55,000 names of men missing (presumed dead) from the conflict at Ypres.

❖ ❖ ❖

The last day of the same month saw the Liverpool Scottish embark upon yet another deadly conflict. The Third Battle of Ypres is better known as the offensive at Passchendale. It turned out to be a terrible and costly encounter for both sides. The Flanders region of Belgium became the key battleground of late summer and autumn 1917. Here, the Allied forces, repelled on many other fronts, hoped to push through and rid Belgium of the German forces. It was also hoped that this would free the Belgian ports of Ostend, Zeebrugge and Bruges, from which many German submarines and other naval craft were attacking Allied ships carrying food and supplies to Britain.

For the Liverpool Scottish, there was a short period of much-needed rest and morale-boosting relaxation before the offensive. The battalion stayed at a friendly village called Zudausques and played some sports. Among the events organized was a cross-country race. Chavasse still had his talent for running and won the race.

But the break was over all too quickly. The offensive started on 31 July with sustained heavy pounding of the German trenches by Allied artillery. The Germans returned fire with explosive shells and shells which dispersed dangerous mustard gas. Chavasse's battalion suffered a number of casualties before they had even reached the front line ready for the attack.

Nevertheless the attack started reasonably well for the Liverpool Scottish, who advanced around 1,828 metres and reached their early targets, despite being held up by some barbed wire at a stream. But then the Germans started to counter-attack with heavy gunfire.

Chavasse moved his first aid post up with the advance, setting it up in a tiny, cramped dugout. (His aim was solely to patch up wounded men before sending them further back to a casualty clearing station.) However, he received an injury when he stood up to show his men where the first aid post was positioned. The splinter from the shell may have fractured his skull; no one is certain. After receiving treatment himself, Chavasse returned to his first aid post and treated men into the evening. As night fell and the rain began, Chavasse continued his work. Carefully, he roamed the fields, using the dim light of an army issue torch to look for injured men.

❖　❖　❖

Early the next day, Chavasse found a German prisoner who happened to be a medic. The man, his name lost to history, worked hard and well with the doctor, and the two of them strived to save and treat seriously wounded men. The German medic was very able and Chavasse was heard to congratulate him on many occasions throughout that long day. The conditions in which they worked were appalling. They operated in a cramped dugout room within the trenches. The filthy mud got absolutely everywhere which made dressing wounds and removing shrapnel and bullets difficult.

As Chavasse left the dugout to call in the next casualty for treatment, a shell flew past him and straight into the room, killing the man he had just been looking after. In the confusion of the battle, no one is quite sure if that was the moment when Chavasse was wounded in the head. But by the end of the day, it is certain that Chavasse had suffered a head wound serious enough to remove him from the front line.

A stretcher-bearer was apparently sent to the aid post to order Chavasse to go back behind the lines. But he insisted that another injured man, a more deserving cause in his opinion, be taken back instead. Late that night, he tried to grab some rest, along with some of the other medical staff. He slept in a chair inside the aid post he worked in, his head aching from its wounds, resting gently on a table.

At around three in the morning, a German shell found the tiny aid post as a target. Many inside the aid post died; the others were so seriously wounded that they could barely move. One of this latter group was Captain Chavasse. He had received four, possibly five wounds from the shell attack to go with the head wounds he had suffered the previous day. The worst wound was one in his body, from which blood poured out. Yet, despite his terrible injuries, Chavasse appeared to be the only one who could remotely move.

In agony, and losing much blood, Chavasse managed to inch his way up the stairs of the aid post and out into the night air. He crawled and staggered his way towards help and found a dugout holding a British lieutenant called Charles Wray. He sent his medics to the first aid post but Chavasse insisted they go and treat his men before they looked at him. None of the others had survived the attack.

Chavasse was carried to a behind-the-lines field hospital unit called Casualty Clearing Station No. 32. It was at a place called Brandhoek and it specialized in wounds to the body, called abdominal wounds. He was operated on at 11 a.m., some eight hours after the attack. The surgeon aimed to remove all the shell fragments and splinters which lay inside his body.

❖ ❖ ❖

The operation appeared successful. Noel woke up and spoke to a Colonel Davidson who reported, 'He seems very weak but spoke cheerfully.' A senior nurse at the casualty clearing station, Sister Ida Leedam, had actually worked with Chavasse at the Southern Hospital in Liverpool. Despite being weak from his terrible wounds, Chavasse recognized her and they talked for a short while.

❖   ❖   ❖

Noel seemed determined that he would pull through, but on 4 August 1917 he died peacefully in his sleep. He was buried the next day and his grave is now at Brandhoek's New Military Cemetery. Naturally, the entire Chavasse family was devastated at the news of his death. His twin brother, Christopher, by now awarded a Military Cross for bravery himself, felt it especially keenly. The tributes flowed thick and fast. There were many letters and telegrams to the Chavasse family, including one from George V, King of England.

In early September, Noel's father learned that his fallen son was to be awarded a second Victoria Cross, known as a Victoria Cross and bar. This made him the only man to win the highest award for gallantry twice in the same war. Only two other men had won the VC twice, and, by a strange quirk of fate, one of those winners was distantly related to the Chavasse family. The other was with the same Field Ambulance unit which took Noel to

Casualty Clearing Station No. 32.

Bishop Chavasse's other two sons fighting for Britain, Bernard and Christopher, both survived the war. Bernard became a famous eye surgeon, while Christopher followed his father into the Church and eventually became Bishop of Rochester. He named his first son Noel, after his brother, and the family tradition of serving bravely continued into the Second World War where the younger Noel won a Military Cross. The end of the citation for Noel Chavasse's second VC is a fitting tribute. It reads: 'By his extraordinary energy and inspiring example he was instrumental in rescuing many wounded who would have otherwise undoubtedly succumbed under the bad weather conditions. This devoted and gallant officer subsequently died of his wounds.'

◆　◆　◆

CHAPTER 6

Never Gave Up

The art of escaping reached its height in World War II, when many captured Allied soldiers, sailors and airmen plotted ingenious ways not just to leave their prison camp but to find a route all the way back to Britain so they could rejoin the fight. Many of them were inspired by the exploits of a tenacious escaper from World War I, A.J. Evans – a man who never, ever gave up.

◆ ◆ ◆

The German rifle muzzle pointed just inches from Evan's head. Looking across at the face of the enemy soldier, Evans knew that he had to stop what he was doing or be shot. Slowly, he dropped the box of matches with which he'd been hoping to set his wrecked aircraft ablaze. He then raised his hands skywards in the universal gesture of surrender. He was a prisoner of the Germans but Evans vowed they wouldn't hold on to him for long.

He was as good as his word.

❖ ❖ ❖

A. J. Evans is barely known today – there are very few books about him. But he was an intrepid fighting man who in 1916 was a member of No. 3 Squadron of the Royal Flying Corps (RFC). A lieutenant and pilot, Evans flew observation and reconnaissance missions over enemy lines. At the start of July 1916, the Somme offensive opened, with thousands of heavy artillery guns launching their shells at enemy targets. The task of spotter planes, like the one Evans was piloting, was to observe where the enemy were positioned. Once this information was sent back, the heavy guns could be trained on those sites.

On 16 July, Evans and his observer, Lieutenant Long, were performing a routine spotting mission when the engine of their aircraft started to give out. They were well behind German lines, with no hope of nursing the aircraft back to safety. As the plane rapidly lost height, Evans looked for a decent place to put the stricken machine down. The only level area suitable for use as a makeshift runway was near large German gun batteries.

There was only one thing for it. Evans knew he had to crash the plane. Skimming the tops of a cluster of trees, Evans dipped the nose of his plane groundwards. Long was almost knocked out by the crash and staggered around the wreckage. Meanwhile, Evans was hanging upside-down from his seat straps and had to wrestle himself free. He then pulled out his matches and searched for the petrol tank of his mashed aircraft, wanting to set his plane ablaze before the Germans arrived so that they couldn't repair it or salvage any of its parts.

❖　❖　❖

Moments after Evans and Long were captured, German officers arrived on the scene. They were about to search the two captured airmen when, to his horror, Evans realized that he had his diary, containing important information, in one of his uniform pockets. He couldn't let this fall into enemy hands. Evans acted coolly. He offered to empty his own pockets and those of Lieutenant Long, still dazed from the crash. He produced everything that the two airmen were carrying except the diary. That was disposed of a little later, dropped secretly into some undergrowth by Evans as the pair were escorted at rifle point to a command post.

Evans was transported to a prisoner of war camp in Gütersloh and then moved on to another camp, this time a converted hotel in the Harz mountains, deep within Germany. At this second camp, Evans made a thorough investigation of the security arrangements and started to plot his escape.

He first joined a team attempting to dig a tunnel out of the camp. Tunnelling was hard, dangerous work with little air reaching the front digger. Evans and others frequently passed out and had to be revived. Day after day, they continued to tunnel but conditions were getting worse and the threat of collapse – and men being buried alive – became too great.

Some involved with the tunnelling gave up the idea of escaping, once their route out had been abandoned. But not Evans. He and a Belgian soldier called Kicq discussed lots of possible plans. Evans spent every spare moment checking the camp for a possible way out and noting the times and directions the sentries patrolled.

The airman spoke reasonable German which certainly helped him get friendly with one of the German guards. He used this friendship to obtain lots of information about trains and travel – a technique used a lot in World War II. He and Kicq bartered, bought and adjusted items of clothing so that they looked like civilians and, finally, they were ready to escape.

❖   ❖   ❖

A small hole in the barbed wire was cut by a comrade and one evening, while the prisoners were still out exercising in the twilight, Evans and Kicq crept through the gap. They froze as the sound of a sentry's footsteps came close. Once the sentry had turned and left the area, the pair ran as fast as they could for as long as they could. Panting and gasping, they listened for any sounds of the alarm being raised. There were none. They had got clear of the camp.

The next stage of their plan was to walk over 16 kilometres to the station at Goslar and board a train for Düsseldorf. There they hoped to bribe a Dutch barge pilot to take them into Holland. From now on, the two acted like strangers to each other. That way, if one was caught, the other might still be able to stay free.

It was an anxious journey on the train. Evans faked being asleep to avoid conversations which might have given him away but kept a lookout for groups of German guards. He got to Düsseldorf but at the docks found only German ships. All alone, Evans had to come up with another plan. He boldly walked into a shop and in his best German asked for a map of the area near the German-Dutch border, explaining that he was on a walking holiday. Amazingly, his nerve held and he got what he wanted. The shopkeeper assumed that no prisoner of war would have the audacity to just walk into a shop in this way.

Evans was tired now but still had to board a tram for Crefeld, the nearest place to the border. From there, he planned to try to walk the 10 or so kilometres to the border. It would be a journey fraught with danger but it was his only hope.

Several nerve-racking tram journeys later, Evans was in Crefeld. He was absolutely worn out now and terribly thirsty but knew he had to keep going. Leaving the town, he stopped from time to time to grab a little liquid by chewing the roots of plants. Many times, the sounds of animals or people forced him to lie low.

It was almost daylight when Evans came within sight of the border. He only had one more stage to go but he knew he had to wait for nightfall to make the final leg. The Englishman crawled along the hilly border territory, trying to work out the best place to make his move. But then disaster struck. He was found by a German soldier.

He tried to pass himself off as a papermaker from another part of Germany but the game was up when he was asked to show his papers. He didn't have any.

As he was marched off, Evans made another desperate bid for freedom. He sprinted away into some woods and kept low to avoid rifle shots. But the wood was bordered by a road, on which another German soldier stood pointing his rifle at Evans.

❖   ❖   ❖

The German soldiers here were not the battle-hardened men of the front. They were older or had some health problem which kept them away from the fighting. They were delighted to realize they had caught an escaped prisoner of war.

Foolishly, they left just one old soldier to guard the prisoner during the night. Evans bided his time and waited. As soon as the guard dozed off, he jumped at the man, knocked him off his feet and flew through the door. He crashed into a sentry and raced on. Within seconds four men were on him, punching and kicking him. One soldier drew his bayonetted rifle and gashed his head.

Beaten and heavily bruised and with blood flowing from his head, Evans was marched to a village called Brüggen where he was questioned for hours. Eventually, Evans was sent all the way back to Clausthal where he had started his escape attempt. He was placed alone in a cramped cell –

solitary confinement being part of his punishment for escaping.

So near and yet so far. Evans had actually got within 20 metres of freedom but he tried not to brood over this near miss. Already, his mind was turning to new ways of getting back to Britain. When he finally rejoined the camp, he was both pleased and saddened to see that Kicq was back as well. Kicq had been on the same train as Evans but found himself in a compartment with a German officer who insisted on chatting to the Belgian. He had been found out not long after.

❖ ❖ ❖

Kicq and Evans were soon moved to a tougher prison camp, one designed to be escape-proof. Based at a place called Ingolstadt on the River Danube, Fort 9, as it was known, was a place for those mainly French, British and Russian servicemen who had attempted to escape before. It was a heavily guarded fortress with a wide moat surrounding the entire camp. The German guards had orders to shoot to kill should they see any prisoner trying to escape.

But within days of arriving, instead of being depressed, Evans was extremely excited. The Germans had herded all those intent on escape into the one place. Compared to other camps, where few prisoners considered such a thing, Fort 9 was teaming with those who had tried and failed but had learned much as a result.

Pooling their knowledge proved a vital key to success – a policy followed at many prisoner of war camps in World War II. Experienced escapers gave lectures to the others, and Evans was delighted to hear their tales. Some had tried to impersonate German officers and had made fake uniforms. Others had smuggled themselves out in rubbish bins. One man had painted his face green and tried to float across the moat, pretending his face was a lily pad!

And it wasn't just information which was passed on at Fort 9. Anyone with a trade taught others or practised their skills themselves to aid escape attempts. Tailors turned parts of military uniforms into convincing civilian clothes, while amateur artists turned their hands to forging documents. A homemade camera was even built and kept hidden from the Germans for taking photos for identity papers.

Evans shared his knowledge and worked for others' escape attempts. He was also involved in a number of attempts himself. He once even tried a dash across the moat, when the winter of 1916 had turned it to ice. Each time he was recaptured and lucky not to be shot.

However, the conditions at Fort 9 got worse and worse as more escape attempts were made. Security was tightened, and privileges removed. Yet, despite all these measures, the camp was proving ungovernable. Eventually, it was learned that the British and Russian prisoners were to be moved to another camp by train. Escaping from a train would be a life-or-death operation but Evans was determined. He teamed up with another prisoner called Buckley who had been at the camp they were heading to. Buckley told Evans it was far worse than Fort 9. The two vowed to make a break for it on the train.

❖ ❖ ❖

The journey from Fort 9 at Ingolstadt to the new camp of Zorndorf took an age. Buckley and Evans were in a compartment with some other British prisoners guarded by one German soldier. However, the corridors and other compartments were full of German soldiers with orders to shoot if they were suspicious. The prisoners established that the guard spoke no English before discussing out loud what they were going to do. There was no way out of the train except through the window.

An opportunity presented itself about 15 kilometres past the German city of Nuremberg. It was now or never. The pair organized a diversion in their compartment. As the train slowed to climb the steep slope, the other prisoners all stood up at the same moment, gathering their bags, pretending that they thought they had reached their destination and blocking the guard's view of the compartment window. In the moment that the guard took his eye off Evans and Buckley, they dived out of the window.

The breath knocked out of them, the two lay where they had hit the hard ground and prayed that the train wouldn't stop. It didn't. Armed with their compasses and some survival rations, the two set off for the border between Germany and Switzerland.

Walking by night, hiding and resting by day, the two covered a staggering 300 kilometres by foot. It took eighteen tension-filled, painful days. Evans' feet were blistered badly after a week and became swollen and sheer agony after ten days. They endured numerous close shaves with both German soldiers and civilians who would have sent out alarms leading to search parties. The two got lost a number of times and their nerves were completely on edge which led to arguments between the pair.

Hunger came close to overcoming them. The meagre rations they carried were quickly exhausted and they couldn't risk trying to enter a village or town. The only food they could find were potatoes dug up by hand from neighbouring fields and eaten raw.

But on the night of the eighteenth day, they got within a whisker of their goal. Ahead of them lay less than a kilometre of German territory before they reached Switzerland. Having got so close to one frontier before, Evans had no intention of making another mistake with this one. The pair spent all day considering the best way to sneak across. Fortunately, it was not as well-guarded as the German-Dutch border, as Switzerland was neutral and had kept out of the war.

On 8 June 1917, Evans and Buckley crept across the border into Switzerland. It was only when spying a noticeboard indicating that they were on neutral soil that the two men finally relaxed. They were dizzy with their success. It was an incredible achievement to have escaped and evaded capture as they had trudged through a vast area of Germany. The two rested in Switzerland for a few days before finally making their way back to England.

❖   ❖   ❖

But Evans hadn't escaped for an easy life. After making his way back to Britain, he insisted on going back into active service. He had to learn how to fly again, as British military aircraft had changed dramatically during his eleven months of captivity.

He was put in charge of training others both in England and Egypt but could not return to the Western Front, as the authorities had decided that no escaped prisoner from one front could return.

Evans finally saw action again by the start of 1918. He was made commander of a bomber squadron in Palestine where the battle still raged against the Turkish forces. Evans loathed bombing but did his duty until 19 March 1918, when, yet again, an engine failure forced him to land and be taken prisoner, this time by the Turkish forces. It goes without saying that he attempted escape from Turkey on a number of occasions.

All in all, by the end of World War I, Evans had spent just under eighteen months as a prisoner or on the run. At no time had the thought of just staying put and sitting out the war seemed to cross his mind. Promoted to the rank of major, Evans put his incredible experiences to good use and in the inter-war years tutored military forces on the art of escape. His 1921 book, The Escaping Club, reads like an adventure yarn but it was all true. It sold so well that it had to be reprinted seven times in just two years.

A world war later, Evans' book and exploits inspired a new generation of prisoners of war to escape.

CHAPTER 7

Crewing a Floating Bomb

While casualties mounted in the land battles in Western Europe, a quite different yet still vital war was being fought at sea in 1917 and 1918. Being an island had saved Britain from invasion in the past, but, as the war progressed, she became more and more dependent on ships to bring food and other supplies. The German submarine fleets, the U-boats, were wreaking havoc. In 1917, almost 4 million tonnes of British, American, Canadian and other Allied countries' merchant shipping was sunk.

Many of the U-boats were based in the heavily guarded triangle of ports of Ostend, Bruges and Zeebrugge. How could they be stopped? The youngest admiral in the Royal Navy proposed an outrageous plan. It required pinpoint accuracy in timing, a massive diversion and a big slice of luck. It became known as the St George's Day raid on Zeebrugge. And one small, yet vital, part of the operation demanded extreme skill and bravery from six men, the crew of the British submarine, the *C3*.

◆ ◆ ◆

Imagine sitting in the cramped confines of a small, elderly submarine as it trawled slowly and dangerously visibly through the waters of the best-guarded harbour in the world at that time. This was the fate of the crew of the British *C3* sub on St George's Day, 23 April 1918.

Almost ten years old, the *C3* was 40 metres long but only 4 metres wide and 3 metres high. It was one of the last submarines to be fitted with ordinary petrol engines. These produced 600 horse-power (not much more than four modern family cars), yet they had to propel 300 tonnes of craft through waters flowing with tides and currents. As a result, the *C3* had a snail-like cruising speed, less than 18 kilometres per hour on the surface and less than 9 kilometres per hour underwater.

In short, the submarine was obsolete. For this

mission, it was also a timebomb. The normal crew of two officers and fourteen crew had been reduced to six in total. The reason – the craft was filled with a powerful explosive, over 5 tonnes of Amatol. One direct hit from the array of guns guarding the port of Zeebrugge and they would be blown sky high.

Their mission was doubly hard because they were supposed to have been partnered by a companion submarine, the *C1*, but it had slipped its towing line too early and was nowhere in sight. The officer in charge of the *C3*, Lieutenant Richard Sandford, and his crew (John Howell-Price, Walter Harner, William Cleaver, Alan Roxburgh and Henry Bendall) were terribly alone, with a deadly task to fulfil. If successful, this single ancient submarine would help put over thirty larger, more advanced enemy subs out of action.

❖　❖　❖

By sinking 400 Allied ships and boats every month, German U-boats were threatening to change the course of the war. In 1917 the British people were trying to get used to having their food rationed. But the British government feared that their country might be starved out of the war before the land campaign in Western Europe could be won. They needed to stop the U-boats reaching the Atlantic and attacking supply ships.

A section of the Royal Navy, called the Dover Patrol, had been in charge of defending the English Channel from attack. They had strung an enormous net across the English Channel and laid minefields on either side of the net. Suspended from fishing boats and buoys, the net was designed to prevent the submarines travelling underwater through the English Channel to attack ships in the Atlantic. But it wasn't working.

Secret documents found on a captured U-boat revealed that the Germans were still passing through the English Channel by surfacing and travelling above the nets and mines at night. From their bases in Belgium and Germany, they simply sailed out into the southernmost part of the North Sea and cruised west through the English Channel, the shortest route to the Atlantic.

The Royal Navy and the military in general were shaken. What could they do to neutralize the U-boat threat? A newly promoted admiral, the youngest in the fleet, had an idea.

A mighty prize – over thirty German submarines and a similar number of German destroyers – lay in the port of Bruges. This Belgian town, occupied by the Germans in the early part of the war, was over 10 kilometres inland and impossible to attack. It was linked to the sea by a large, heavily guarded canal system which ran past two further Belgian ports, Ostend and Zeebrugge. Attempting to capture any of the three ports would be madness. They were defended by massive sets of fortifications with over 220 artillery guns and thousands of well-equipped soldiers.

But could a part of the waterway linking the ports to the sea be blocked? The 45-year-old Admiral Roger Keyes thought so. He targeted the port of Zeebrugge and fought long and hard to persuade other admirals that his plan should be attempted.

❖ ❖ ❖

In the spring of 1918, Keyes' plan, codenamed Operation ZO, was almost complete. It was a complicated sequence of actions, all of which had to be performed well for the raid to be successful. Three ancient naval cruisers, the *Iphigenia*, the *Thetis* and the *Intrepid*, filled with concrete, were to be sunk in the waters of Zeebrugge, blocking the way out to the sea. To get them close enough, a massive diversion was needed. This was to be provided by a giant smokescreen deployed by some of the vessels, and an attack on the gigantic harbour wall surrounding part of Zeebrugge.

The harbour wall, known as a mole, was almost 2 kilometres in length and the largest of its kind in the world. Made from stone, steel and granite, it stood over 10 metres high in places and was wide enough to carry a rail track, a paved road and a walkway for soldiers. It was home to around a thousand German soldiers and needed to be attacked directly. Troops from HMS *Vindictive* and from two Mersey ferry boats, the *Iris* and the *Daffodil*, were to board the mole, and destroy as many of the large German artillery guns there as possible. These troops and the skeleton crews of the three sunken ships would be recovered as soon as the ships blocked the port.

To prevent hefty German reinforcements coming from land, the harbour wall was to be cut off by destroying the viaduct which connected it to the mainland. This was the task of Sandford and the rest of the crew of the *C3* submarine.

Their high-risk mission was simple but deadly. Their craft was to sail under the viaduct and be blown up. But just getting in position was fraught with danger. The six-man crew of the *C3* understood this all too well as they were towed from British shores by the Royal Navy destroyer *Trident* on the evening of 23 April 1918.

❖ ❖ ❖

The tension was unbearable as Lieutenant Sandford skippered the *C3* into the waters near Zeebrugge. Their mission partner, the *C1*, had failed to show. It was all up to them. The smoke-screen had already been laid (by means of injecting chemicals into the exhaust fumes of smaller motor boats), and the landing party attacks by Marines and Royal Navy troops were under way. More than 2 kilometres of open water lay between the *C3* and its target, and the submarine had to travel this distance on the surface, as the water was too shallow for a stealthier, underwater approach.

The *C3* chugged infuriatingly slowly towards its target. All the crew were aware of how easily they could be caught in the glare of searchlights and flashes from the battle. A moment's bad luck and they would become a sitting target, whilst all the time they sat on tonnes of deadly explosives. The tension was extreme, the mission tougher than any the six men had ever experienced before.

❖ ❖ ❖

The situation got even worse when a shift in wind direction moved the smokescreen away. From the shoreline and the mole, the *C3* showed up as a murky, grey object in the water. Suddenly, search-lights were cast down and shells pounded the water around the submarine.

Miraculously, the *C3* wasn't hit. The crew stuck to their task. They all had great faith in their popular and experienced commander, Lieutenant

Sandford. A navy man since joining as a cadet in 1904, he had spent his entire wartime service in underwater shipping.

Sandford had the agreement of his crew when he went against the orders he'd been given. The crew were supposed to leave the submarine in their two dinghies, known as skiffs, a few hundred metres short of the viaduct. The idea was that the submarine's gyro-compass would then steer the unmanned vessel into the viaduct. But Sandford believed that this was too risky. The six men hadn't come this far not to guarantee a successful mission. They stayed aboard the craft to the very end.

As the *C3* veered towards the viaduct, its crew stood on the deck. The six men held on tight as their vessel lumbered into the viaduct and lodged right into the structure's supports. The Germans assumed that the submarine was attempting to enter the harbour and they had relaxed as it progressed. They were convinced that it would wreck itself or get stuck and would be easily captured a little later.

❖ ❖ ❖

Sandford set the explosives with their five-minute fuse and the crew attempted to retreat. One of their skiffs had disappeared, so the six men prepared to cram themselves into the one remaining escape craft. The waters were choppy and unsteady and the Germans were a short distance away as they launched their dinghy. Its propeller struck the body of the submarine and snapped off. The dinghy's small engine was now useless. The men would have to try and row for it.

Fighting the strong swirls of water, they slowly started to put distance between themselves and the deadly submarine. Harner and Bendall took the oars first, fighting the currents and making painfully slow progress. The Germans cottoned on to the attempted escape. Shots rang out in the night air.

Sandford was hit, first in the hand and then in the thigh. Another volley of rifle shots headed towards the small dinghy. Bendall and Harner were both hit by German fire. Cleaver took up an oar before he was shot almost immediately. Bendall caught another bullet. Sandford's second-in-command, Howell-Price, and Roxburgh grabbed the oars from their fallen comrades and rowed with all their remaining energy.

❖ ❖ ❖

Suddenly an enormous explosion tore the air. The explosives aboard the *C3* had successfully detonated. The viaduct was ripped apart by the blast. Large and small chunks of masonry rained into the water. The sub's crew were not much more than 200 metres away from the explosion and were lucky not to be hit by the debris.

Shortly after, a small 16 metre long vessel, called a picket boat, came into view. It was the smallest British craft in the whole raid on Zeebrugge and was skippered by Richard Sandford's elder brother, Francis. The crew of the *C3* were hoisted aboard and then transferred to a larger vessel, HMS *Phoebe*, so the injured could be treated. Francis Sandford then piloted his boat back into the thick of the action to try to rescue others. Despite sustaining engine damage, Francis Sandford's small craft eventually managed to limp back home to Britain.

Amazingly, considering their injuries, the entire six-man crew of the *C3* made it back to Britain alive. All were decorated. Sandford was awarded the Victoria Cross, his second-in-command, Lieutenant Howell-Price, received the Distinguished Service Order (DSO) and the other four received the Conspicuous Gallantry Medal (CGM). But tragedy was to strike the *C3*'s commander shortly after his recommendation for the Victoria Cross in July 1918. On 23 November 1918, twelve days after the armistice ending World War I was signed, Richard Sandford died of pneumonia.

❖　❖　❖

Long before Richard Sandford's death, the St George's Day raid on Zeebrugge was heralded as a great success by the British government and military.

'The raid on Zeebrugge may well rank as the finest feat of arms in the Great War, and certainly as an episode unsurpassed in the history of the Royal Navy,' said the MP, Winston Churchill who would become Prime Minister of Britain in World War II.

The Prime Minister at the time, David Lloyd George, was just as enthusiastic. Exploits like this one helped to boost the morale of a public desperate for a daring success and weary of the huge casualties in the long-running land war in Western Europe.

❖   ❖   ❖

The story of the *C3*'s crew is just one of dozens of tales of incredible heroism shown by those aboard the ships, those soldiers who landed and fought on the mole, and those who attempted to rescue the attackers when the raid was in retreat. But sadly, despite the intense gallantry of many of those involved, the operation was ultimately a failure. The 214 killed and 383 wounded participants of Operation ZO did not completely succeed in blocking the waterway at Zeebrugge. The three concrete-laden ships were sunk, but not in the correct position. And, within forty-eight hours, German forces were dredging and clearing the channel of wreckage, enabling many of the U-boats to go back out to sea again.

◆ ◆ ◆

The Red Battle Flyer

By the time the war on the Western Front reached its third year, the public and press on both sides were despondent at the high casualties and seeming lack of progress. Governments and military officials therefore attempted to raise public morale by focusing on heroic endeavours and notable successes. From this point of view, the war in the air was very appealing. It appeared to be glamorous and chivalrous – pilots in air combat were almost like medieval knights jousting to the death – a far cry from the squalid conditions and massive death toll of the disease-ridden trenches of the Western Front. Both sides touted their own flying heroes and the notion of aces – pilots who had downed a significant number of enemy aircraft – was born.

The most famous ace of World War I was undoubtedly Manfred von Richthofen. To the French he was known as the Red Devil, and to the British as the Red Baron. But the German people, who revelled in his ability to shoot down enemy aircraft seemingly at will, knew him by the title of his 1917 memoirs, as the Red Battle Flyer.

◆ ◆ ◆

Manfred von Richthofen gripped the control column of his fighter plane and plunged it downwards at high speed. He was locked in combat with a deadly adversary, one whose skill and experience appeared to be finding their mark.

It was 23 November 1916 and the 24-year-old fighter pilot had only been in action for a couple of months. He held all the advantages. His plane, an Albatross, was around 30 kilometres per hour faster than the Allied DH2 aircraft he was fighting, and they were over German lines. Yet, from the start of their private battle, when the pilot of the British plane had given a contemptuous wave, von Richthofen was aware that he was dealing with the best enemy pilot he had encountered.

Dogfights were usually fast and furious, finished in a few minutes, but this titanic struggle lasted over half an hour. Both men wheeled, climbed and dived their planes around the skies, looking for that one lethal opening which would signal the end of their adversary. The British aircraft started to run low on fuel. Its pilot broke away from the dogfight and started to head home at speed. Von Richthofen pounced. As the DH2 zig-zagged in front of him, Richthofen waited and waited until the plane crossed his gunsights at suitably close range. Then, and only then, did he unleash a furious burst from his plane's machine guns.

The British pilot was killed instantly. His aircraft veered to the side, out of control, and crashed into a ruined building. Von Richthofen had recorded his eleventh victory by shooting down Lanoe Hawker – at the time, the greatest British fighter ace. The career of the Red Battle Flyer had been well and truly launched.

❖   ❖   ❖

Manfred Albrecht Freiherr von Richthofen was born into an aristocratic German family on 2 May 1892 in the town of Breslau (now the Polish town of Wroclaw). His father was one of the first Richthofens to embark upon a military career. He wished his eldest son (Manfred had an elder sister and two younger brothers) to follow in his foot-steps, and he insisted on eleven-year-old Manfred enrolling as a military cadet at a Prussian academy based at Wahlstatt.

The young Manfred had already developed a fascination for hunting and guns, partly inspired by his military father but truly ignited by visits from his uncle, Alexander von Schickfuss, his mother's brother. Uncle Alexander was a wealthy and dedicated hunter of wild animals. He had travelled the world shooting big game such as lions, tigers and even elephants. Visits to Uncle Alexander's home to see the heads of the exotic creatures he had killed, and the weaponry he had used, inspired his young nephew to practise and become a crack shot with an air rifle.

Manfred didn't care for the strict, rather dull regime at the cadet school. He did just enough to scrape through tests and was considered a very average pupil. However, he loved sports and gymnastics and thrived on taking risks even at an early age. Before he had reached his teens, the young cadet had risked life and limb climbing the famous church steeple at Wahlstatt. Von Richthofen tied his handkerchief to the steeple's lightning conductor rod, just for fun. Ten years later, when visiting his younger brother, Lothar, at the cadet school, Manfred could still spy the tattered remains of his handkerchief fluttering there.

❖　❖　❖

Two years before World War I started, von Richthofen joined the German Cavalry as a junior officer. He was twenty years old and had great energy and strength. But his piercing blue eyes and abrupt manner gave the impression of coldness, and he was remembered in the cavalry for his efficiency rather than his friendliness.

At the start of the war, his cavalry force was posted to Germany's border with Russia, before being switched to a supporting position on the Western Front. Behind the front line, the lack of action told on von Richthofen. He was bored by the inactivity and, having seen the German observation planes in the skies, put in for a transfer to the German Flying Service. Following his first test flight in May 1915, von Richthofen was posted to the Russian front as an observer in slow, unarmed German reconnaissance planes.

❖   ❖   ❖

By the autumn of the same year, he was back on the Western Front. He was still an observer but now had a single machine gun to control for the plane's defence. Richthofen managed to down an enemy spotter aircraft with his single machine gun but it was a chance meeting which set him on the path to becoming the war's leading fighter ace. Sitting in a train compartment, Richthofen started talking to

Oswald Boelcke, one of the first great German aces of the war. The conversation inspired von Richthofen to train as a fighter pilot.

❖ ❖ ❖

Von Richthofen was, if anything, a below average trainee. His handling of the controls was stiff and rigid, and on his first solo flight he crashed his aircraft – although he escaped unharmed. Gradually, however, he gained confidence and skill and finally qualified.

His timing was fortunate. The German ace he had met on the train, Oswald Boelcke, had been put in charge of an elite air force and was looking to recruit pilots. Von Richthofen joined JASTA 2 in the summer of 1916. In September of the same year, Boelcke's unit shot down twenty-five enemy aircraft for the loss of only three of their own planes. Von Richthofen was among the victors, notching up his first kill.

Von Richthofen's tally mounted fast and the downing of Lanoe Hawker, his eleventh victory, greatly added to his reputation. In January 1917 he became commander of his own unit of aircraft known as JASTA 11. In the same month he received a much-prized medal called the 'Pour le Mérite' but better known as the Blue Max. He was so proud of this decoration that he wore it every day in combat.

Von Richthofen had no interest in the other roles being assigned to aircraft as World War I progressed, such as spotting artillery positions or bombing enemy airfields and troop positions. In his words, 'The duty of the fighting pilot is to patrol his area of the sky, and shoot down any enemy fighters in that area. Anything else is rubbish.'

❖ ❖ ❖

In June 1917, the German air force was reorganized into four large groups of aircraft. Richthofen was in charge of one of these units, still known as JASTA 11. Shortly after, he painted his aircraft red and other pilots in his force also daubed their planes in bright colours. Von Richthofen's 'Flying Circus' was born.

In the winter of 1917, a brand new German fighter plane was rolled out in Berlin. It was a three-winged aircraft, or triplane, known as the Fokker DR1 Dreidecker. Von Richthofen was given the chance to test the compact aircraft out and was impressed. He commented that, 'It climbed like a monkey and manoeuvred like the devil'.

His force was the first to receive the new aircraft. Just like his earlier Albatross fighter plane, von Richthofen painted his new craft bright red. The sight of the plane in the sky a long distance away was enough to fill enemy pilots with dread. If they chanced upon the red triplane at close quarters, dread would turn to naked terror, especially for the large numbers of new Allied pilots being pressed into service.

Not that von Richthofen was allowed free, safe passage through the skies. On the contrary, he was the greatest possible prize for the many experienced French, British, Canadian, Australian and American pilots. He was shot at countless times, and in the summer of 1917 received a bullet in the head which blinded him. Somehow, von Richthofen managed to steer his plane to the ground before collapsing. He required two operations to remove bone splinters from his head and suffered incredibly intense headaches before returning to active service just five weeks after the near-death encounter.

❖　❖　❖

At the start of 1918, von Richthofen's tally of kills topped sixty. He had been showered with decorations and glory by the German authorities. His superiors in the military and many senior politicans were desperate for him to retire. But he had become such a hero to the German people that the thought of losing him was too much to bear. At the same time, von Richthofen was too public a figure to be forced to retire if he didn't want to.

Meanwhile, von Richthofen himself was becoming tired of the war and depressed at the rising death toll. He once said, 'I think of this war as it really is, not as the people at home imagine, with a hoorah! and a roar. It is very serious, very grim.'

Yet he had no interest in taking a desk job far from the action. As long as there were German troops fighting in the trenches, Richthofen maintained that he would continue the war in the air.

And continue he did. Despite the Allied forces receiving new, higher-performance aircraft, von Richthofen still notched up victory after victory. Between 12 March and 20 April 1918, he managed to down another thirteen aircraft. His tally was now eighty.

❖ ❖ ❖

The patrol on 21 April 1918 started just like most other patrols for the Flying Circus. The pilots in the unit included Manfred von Richthofen in search of his eighty-first kill, and also his cousin Wolfram von Richthofen on his very first combat flight. Wolfram was under orders from his illustrious cousin to avoid fighting at all costs.

On the opposing side, a Canadian pilot, Wilfred May (known as 'Wop' to his friends), was embarking on his very first combat patrol under pretty much the same set of orders. He was flying a

Sopwith Camel from 209 Squadron and had spent much of the previous day picking up tips and advice from his old schoolfriend who happened to be a senior figure in the same squadron, Captain Roy Brown.

The two units met in the sky over the British and Australian lines near the Somme and an enormous dogfight began. May circled at high altitude above the action but could not restrain himself when he saw a Fokker watching the battle just like him. May managed to fire a burst of bullets at the silver-bodied Fokker triplane. The aircraft, believed to be Wolfram von Richthofen's, was hit in the tail and limped its way back to base. May was delighted to have had a stab at the enemy, and when his guns jammed a few moments later he decided to head back to base, pleased with his work.

Within a couple of minutes his pleasure had turned to terror. Behind him swooped a dark red Fokker Triplane. It was Manfred von Richthofen's craft and it was closing fast.

May pushed his control column forward and dived. The German aircraft followed him. Back among the mêlée of aircraft, Captain Brown spotted his old schoolfriend's plight, cursed, and wheeled away to give chase.

May was getting desperate. His plane and the German aircraft pursuing him were no more than

70 metres from the ground and still he could not get free. A hail of bullets spluttered from the Fokker's twin machine guns. Many of them started to rip into the wings and fuselage of May's aircraft. Diving down, Brown managed to get the red triplane in his gunsights for a brief moment. He let go a burst of fire from his Vickers machine guns but his path took him below the two aircraft he was chasing and when he levelled out and rose again, May and von Richthofen were nowhere to be seen.

❖ ❖ ❖

For a full minute after Brown's attack, Manfred von Richthofen's aircraft continued to chase and close in on May's stricken Sopwith Camel. The Canadian wrenched his control column this way and that, trying to twist and turn his craft away from his pursuer. Behind him, von Richthofen seemed to read and follow his every move. The Red Baron appeared to be closing in for his eighty-first kill.

At an altitude of no more than 25 metres, the two aircraft were flying incredibly low over Allied lines, so low that the Sopwith Camel's wheels clipped the tops of a clump of trees at one point. Moments later, they passed straight over the heads of Australian gunners manning posts by the Somme. Several fired at the red triplane, most notably Sergeant Cedric Popkin and two anti-aircraft gunners in the Australian Imperial Force, Private Snowy Evans and Private Robert Buie. All three believed that they hit the aircraft and possibly the pilot, but what is certain is that shortly afterwards the red triplane crash-landed, skidding to a halt on some high ground above the Somme waterway.

Ground forces who had followed the battle in the air raced to the scene. They found Baron Manfred von Richthofen still in his cockpit but quite dead. He was twenty-five years old. Much of the aircraft was stripped as the soldiers fought excitedly for souvenirs, but von Richthofen's body was treated with due respect. It was carried to an Allied medical facility where doctors performed two autopsies in order to find out exactly how he had died.

Von Richthofen was found to have had his nose and jaw broken from the impact of the crash but what had killed him was a single bullet which had entered his back and pierced his heart. Both the Australian soldiers on the ground and the Canadian pilot Roy Brown claimed the bullet was one of theirs and, to some extent, the mystery rumbles on to this day.

Many believe that the Red Baron could not have continued to fly his aircraft with the skill and accuracy he appeared to manage for a whole minute after the machine gun burst from Captain

Brown's aircraft. The most likely explanation is that ground fire accounted for von Richthofen's demise. Yet the Royal Flying Corps had become the Royal Air Force on 1 April 1918 and it was important for the new air force to claim the invincible Red Baron's scalp for themselves.

❖   ❖   ❖

The next day, von Richthofen was buried with full military honours. Judging from the procession and ceremony, it almost appeared as if the Allies were burying one of their own heroes, such was the respect accorded to World War I's Ace of Aces. (However, von Richthofen was eventually re-buried back in Germany in 1925 in an elaborate ceremony involving the then President, Field Marshal von Hindenburg.)

News filtered back to the Flying Circus's base the evening of the day of Richthofen's death, although this was not officially confirmed until 23 September. All the pilots, engineers and personnel of von Richthofen's force were devastated, his younger brother, Lothar, and cousin, Wolfram, especially so. The loss of Germany's greatest fighter pilot was a bitter blow to German morale at a time when the war in Europe was not going well.

But the entire Flying Circus continued the fight, spurred on by a desire to avenge their fallen leader.

By the war's end, JASTA 11 had notched up hundreds of victories in total and had found a new figurehead in Ernst Udet, the surviving fighter pilot with the most kills – sixty-two. The Red Baron's younger brother, Lothar, survived the war with an impressive forty downed enemy aircraft to his credit.

Attempts to belittle Manfred von Richthofen's achievements soon started, and continued long after his death and the end of World War I. Many have questioned how one man could have shot down so many aircraft, and have pointed to his interest in glory and decorations to hint that his claims were exaggerated.

However, a look at Manfred von Richthofen's service record provides many of the answers. He was an exceptionally experienced pilot who had been flying in one form or another from 1915 until his death in April 1918, much longer than most flyers of the Great War. In addition to his natural talent and intuition as a hunter and marksman, he had been trained by the cream of German pilots, particularly the first great fighter ace, Oswald Boelcke. Von Richthofen doubled his mentor's tally of kills, and he remains, without question, the most famous and revered fighter pilot of World War I.

◆　◆　◆

CHAPTER 9

Leading from the Front

The United States officially entered the war on the side of the British, French and other Allied forces in the spring of 1917. But it was only the following year that troops of the American Expeditionary Force (AEF) arrived in the numbers required to make a difference. The AEF soldiers were under overall Allied command in a number of battles but the first full-scale American-led attack was the St Mihiel offensive in September 1918. It proved to be part of a crucial campaign which swung the war on Europe's Western Front in favour of the Allies.

The man in charge of America's first unit of tanks was a 32-year-old lieutenant colonel called

George S. Patton Junior. A man of action, Patton would later become most famous as a general in World War II. But, during the St Mihiel offensive, and against the wishes of his superiors, Patton led from the front with great success.

◆ ◆ ◆

On 6 April 1917, the United States Congress and the President of the United States, Woodrow Wilson, declared war on Germany. At the time, the United States had a relatively small army, numbering under 200,000, which mainly guarded its borders. Then the Selective Service Act was passed, requiring all American men between the ages of twenty-one and thirty to register for military service. In total, about four million men were drafted into the US military, of which around half served overseas.

The force included around 200,000 African-American soldiers, of whom 42,000 were combat troops. Yet, as in most of American society at the time, blacks and whites were kept apart under a policy called segregation. The African-American soldiers actually fought with the French Army during World War I. By May 1918, just over half a million American soldiers had arrived in Europe.

Within a couple of months, that number had

doubled. The entire force was under the control of General John Joseph Pershing. General Pershing was the United States' most experienced military commander. A former schoolteacher, he had spent twelve years fighting Native American tribes including the Sioux and the Apache. He had also fought in the Cuban war of 1898 and with the Japanese Army in their 1904-5 war against Russia. He was one of the few high-ranking American soldiers who had recently led troops in battle prior to reaching Europe. In 1916, he led an expedition into Mexico to attack the notorious bandit leader, Pancho Villa.

❖　❖　❖

One of Pershing's personal aides was George Smith Patton Junior. Patton had grown up in California and, although his father's business fortunes varied, the family had a comfortable life. The young George, as he was known, spent a happy childhood. He was particularly fond of riding horses and had entered America's famous military academy, West Point, in 1904.

Despite suffering from dyslexia, which made it hard for him to read or spell, he graduated from West Point in 1909. His class included three men who would later become full generals themselves, William Hood Simpson, Jacob Devers and Robert

Lawrence Eichelberger. Having married his sweetheart, Beatrice, in 1910, Patton took part in the 1912 Olympic Games in Stockholm, Sweden. He came fifth in the pentathlon before resuming his military career.

As part of Pershing's force in Mexico, Patton assisted the General in planning but wanted to get into the thick of the action himself. He badgered his senior officers until he was given temporary charge of an active unit.

On 14 May 1916, he led a small force which chased a group of bandits to a Mexican farmhouse. Pistol drawn, Patton led from the front, bobbing and weaving towards the farmhouse. Suddenly, three Mexican bandits on horseback sped towards him, firing their guns.

Astonishingly, Patton managed to shoot the first two men off their horses. The third dismounted to get a better aim at the American soldier but missed. Patton shot him as well. The three dead Mexicans were strapped to Patton's car and he drove off to General Pershing's headquarters. It turned out that the third Mexican Patton had shot was one of Pancho Villa's most senior lieutenants. Pershing praised Patton himself and the event was reported in the newspapers back in the United States.

❖   ❖   ❖

The General took Patton with him as a valued aide when the AEF headed to France in 1917. But Patton soon grew frustrated by the lack of action and, again, pestered his commander to move him to a front-line force. Eventually, Pershing gave in and Patton received a prize transfer – he was to command the United States' first tank unit.

The Somme, in September 1916, had seen the first use of tanks in battle. The British Mark 1s used there were quickly followed by improved British and French designs. Yet, until November 1917, tank warfare had achieved little real success. World War I tanks were not the sophisticated machines we know today. Lightly armed, they were mainly used to breach barriers of barbed wire and other obstacles as foot soldiers advanced. The tanks were unreliable and dreadfully slow, rarely moving faster than 10 kilometres per hour. In the muddy conditions of many areas on the Western Front, they often got bogged down.

The Battle of Cambrai, in November 1917, was the first time tanks were used in their hundreds. It was also their first success. In a surprise attack, over 8,000 German prisoners were taken and 100 gun positions captured.

Patton watched, fascinated, from inside one of the 378 British tanks at Cambrai, wanting to learn all about this new type of warfare. He also visited other British and French tank units and became excited by the possibilities tanks offered but also mindful of their dangers.

He spent long hours training his unit and became known as a hard taskmaster. Incredibly strict on discipline, Patton didn't set out to be liked by his soldiers, just trusted and followed. He never asked his men to do anything he wouldn't do himself, and over time he earned their unwavering respect. His force were eventually equipped with a French tank called the Renault FT17. Weighing over 7 tonnes, it was still a fraction of the size and weight of the larger British tanks and had fewer armaments but was easier to manoeuvre. It's absolute top speed was 9.7 kilometres per hour.

❖   ❖   ❖

During the winter and spring of 1917/18, while Patton trained his tank units, American soldiers fought alongside the Allies, defending parts of the Western Front from attempted advances by the Germans. In May 1918, many soldiers from the AEF joined Allied attacks under the command of British or French Generals at Canal du Nord and Le Hamel. But Pershing was keen to wrestle command of the increasingly large American forces away from foreigners and back to himself. By the end of August 1918, he had got his way. The renamed

First American Army was under his command.

The First American Army's first target was an area known as the St Mihiel salient. A salient is a bulge in a line between two opposing armed forces. The soldiers in a salient have the disadvantage of facing the enemy on two or three sides. Sometimes this can encourage enemy attacks; the Ypres salient, for example, saw much action throughout World War I. But the St Mihiel salient had been relatively quiet since 1916. The Germans had actually started to use the area as a place for new or resting, battle-weary troops.

Pershing assembled a large force of some 300,000 personnel but the German High Command somehow learned of the planned attack and started to withdraw. The offensive needed to be swift, so on 12 September Pershing ordered his forces forward. After artillery bombardment, the first wave of American troops and tank units started to move out at 5 a.m.

❖   ❖   ❖

As they slowly advanced over the muddy ground, things started to go wrong. A few tanks got stuck but the main problem seemed to be lack of experience. Most of the tank unit personnel hadn't fought before and the infantry were not used to working alongside these new machines. On a number of occasions, the tanks rumbled forward, unaware that they were leaving the infantry they were designed to aid a long way behind.

With no radio contact between tanks and commanders, all Patton and other officers could rely on was a system of runners. These were soldiers entrusted with the risky task of passing orders and commands by hand through the battle lines. Back at a command point, Patton could see the problems but, from his position, he was powerless to influence the situation, even via runners. Senior officers were expected to hang back and view the battle from a safe distance. In a painfully slow infantry advance this may have been possible, but the attack was relatively rapid. Patton knew he had to join his men, even though it was against orders.

Racing down to the battlefield on foot through the clinging mud, dodging enemy shells, Patton got right into the thick of the action. He took shelter behind a small ridge and analysed the battle. He saw some of the German forces heading back to a village called Essey. Running to where one of his unit commanders stood, he ordered five tanks to be sent into the village. Patton accompanied them, walking with the tanks and, for a time, leading them on foot.

They came to a bridge which looked hazardous but Patton walked straight across it, braving fire from enemy snipers nearby. The tanks followed and made their way into the village. After a short exchange of fire, the five tanks quickly overwhelmed the Germans, who surrendered.

❖ ❖ ❖

Patton and his tanks had secured a key target but they couldn't rest on their laurels. He asked and received permission to advance north-west to the village of Pannes. Again he led from the front, walking ahead of his tanks and risking his own life in order to secure their next objective. The road from Essey to Pannes was littered with the dead bodies of German soldiers and many of the American infantrymen accompanying Patton's group of tanks were horrified by what they saw. To reassure them, Patton insisted that he would enter the village with a tank first.

Perched on top of one of the Renault FT17s as it moved forward, Patton became a target for the Germans in the village. Machine-gun and rifle fire raked the side of the tank, narrowly missing Patton. He was forced to take cover. Leaping off the tank, he rolled into a shellhole. The tank continued to trundle on and the infantry was still a long way behind. Patton was dangerously isolated, several hundred metres from both the tanks and the infantry, but he was more concerned for the crew of his tank who were now on their own.

Finding his way back to the infantry by jumping from shellhole to shellhole, Patton urged them to advance but their commanders refused. Then Patton asked for a runner from the infantry to reach his tank and order it back. Again, he was met with a refusal. Patton now had to act as his own runner, dodging yet more fire to chase the tank and order its return. Eventually, another advance was arranged, with infantry and tanks together, and Pannes was seized.

❖　❖　❖

Night fell, with gains of more than 7 kilometres, but Patton didn't rest. Instead, he crept back from the front line to secure more fuel for his tanks. They were back in action and over the next couple of days made further gains. Patton had trained his tank unit commanders well. A number acted quickly and successfully on their own initiative when faced with deadly situations and were decorated with medals.

By 16 September, the entire St Mihiel salient was under Allied control and the tanks had played a vital part. Not that this stopped Patton from receiving the most enormous telling-off. His immediate superior, Brigadier General Samuel D. Rockenbach, was furious that Patton had left his safe command post to join his tanks on the front line. Fortunately, a note arrived from the very top of the First American Army. General Pershing had learned of Patton's actions and congratulated him. As tank warfare progressed, it became clear that commanders had to be closer to the action to have any hope of controlling it.

❖ ❖ ❖

After a week's rest, Patton and his tanks were again in action as the American forces launched their second major offensive in a fortnight. This time, the Americans were to attack the Germans from the south in an area bounded by the Argonnes forest and the River Meuse. Again, Patton found himself having to lead from the front.

Some of the trenches were too deep for the Renault tanks to cross but Patton was not going to be stopped. Picking up a shovel, he started to fill an area of the trench himself, despite being a target for enemy fire. Inspired by his example, many of his men joined in and soon a break in the trench system had been created for some of the tanks to rumble through. The battlefield was chaotic and many infantrymen were dazed and petrified. Shifting waves of fog and smoke only added to the confusion. But Patton did his best to keep control and urge American soldiers onward.

Patton was keen to locate the position of several German machine-gun nests which were sweeping the land with fire. Walking ahead of the tanks with a few men, Patton and his loyal aide, Lieutenant Angelo, pressed on, even though soldiers around them were being mown down by enemy rifles and machine guns. Suddenly, Patton's aide watched in horror as his commander fell, hit by a bullet in his thigh.

Angelo dragged Patton into an empty shellhole for cover and tried to stem the heavy flow of blood from the wound. Patton had been badly hurt by the bullet but remained just about conscious and was able to pass on the location of one of the enemy machine gun sites to his tank forces. His loyal lieutenant insisted on staying by Patton's side, despite the top of the shellhole being ripped apart by German bullets.

Hours later, once the German machine gun posts had been silenced, Patton was finally rescued and taken back to a first aid station. Stubborn as ever, he insisted on a detour to divisional head-quarters to give his report before giving up his command and being operated on. When he came round the following day, he was shown a newspaper with the headline 'America's Tank Hero'. Patton was well on his way to becoming a legend.

❖   ❖   ❖

With enormous casualties, the Argonnes-Meuse offensive was not as clear a success as the St Mihiel attack had been. Progress remained slow and casualties grew but Allied forces were now advancing in many areas of the Western Front, and, a little over a month later, Germany surrendered. Patton recovered from his wound in time to witness the Armistice signed on 11 November 1918. His role in World War I was over, but he would forge a reputation as a fearless senior general over twenty years later in World War II.

Glossary

Allies almost thirty countries, including Britain, France, Australia, South Africa, Canada, India, New Zealand, Japan, Belgium, Serbia and the United States, which fought the Central Powers.

altitude the height above the ground that an aircraft travels at.

amphibious vehicle/landing a vehicle that works, or a military operation that occurs, both on land and in water.

artillery large guns used on land to fire shells at enemy positions.

battalion a large section of an armed force on land, made up of many hundreds of soldiers.

bayonet a knife blade fitted to the end of a gun.

border the boundary line between two countries.

camouflage ways of painting and disguising soldiers, bases and military equipment to make them hard for the enemy to spot.

cavalry units of soldiers on horseback.

Central Powers those countries, including Germany, Austria-Hungary, the Ottoman Empire (Turkey), and Bulgaria, which fought the Allies in World War I.

chlorine gas dangerous gas used in World War I which damages and destroys the lungs.

diversion a military move to attract enemy attention to one area while a more important military operation occurs in another.

dogfight a fight between two or more aircraft.

dugout a roofed shelter in part of a trench.

dysentery a potentially fatal disease of the digestive system.

evacuation to withdraw or move people from one place to another, safer place.

fugitives people who flee from the authorities. Escaped prisoners of war in enemy territory were fugitives.

gallantry bravery.

garrison a fortress or other building that houses soldiers used to defend a town.

infantry soldiers who march, move and fight on foot.

mobilize to assemble and prepare soldiers for war.

morale the mood or confidence of soldiers or the public.

mustard gas German-developed chemical weapon – a gas which could get through clothing, damaging eyes and blistering skin.

No Man's Land contested area of ground between two enemy forces.

offensive a major attack, involving many soldiers, on an enemy's line.

propaganda the use of speeches, newspapers and other media to influence people's attitudes and emotions. Anti-enemy propaganda was common in World War I.

rationing fixing daily or weekly allowances of different foods.

reconnaissance an inspection or exploration of an area, especially one made to gather military information.

recruitment getting people to join up and fight in the armed forces.

reinforcements extra troops and equipment sent to join a military force.

retreat withdraw and go back into safer territory.

sentry a soldier acting as a guard, protecting an area or person.

shells hollow metal or paper cases containing explosives and fired from large artillery guns.

shellholes craters in the ground caused by exploding shells. Shellholes could be deep enough to provide hiding places for soldiers.

shrapnel fragments of bombs and pieces of metal thrown out from an explosion.

snipers hidden soldiers firing from long range at individual enemy soldiers.

volunteers people who offer to perform a task or join the armed forces without being ordered to by the authorities.

◆ ◆ ◆

Further reading

Chapter 1:
Fighter Heroes of WWI, Joshua Levine,
Collins, 2011

Chapter 2:
Jacka CV: Australian Hero, Robert Macklin,
Allen & Unwin Pty Ltd, 2006

Chapter 3:
Edith Cavell: Nurse, Martyr, Heroine, Diana Souhami,
Quercus, 2011

Chapter 4:
Lawrence of Arabia, Alistair MacLean,
Sterling Juvenile, 2007

Chapter 5:
Noel Chavasse Double VC, Ann Clayton,
Pen & Sword Military, 2006
A detailed biography of the life of Noel Chavasse with
photographs can be found at Ian Jones's excellent website:
www.chavasse.u.net.com/chavasse.html

Chapter 6:

Tunnelling to Freedom: And Other Escape Narratives from World War I, Hugh Durnford
Dover Publications Ltd, 2004

Chapter 7:

Blocking of Zeebrugge, Stephen Price,
Osprey Publishing, 2010

Chapter 8:

The Red Fighter Pilot: The Autobiography of the Red Baron, Manfred von Richthofen, Red & Black Publishers, 2013

Chapter 9:

Tanks and Trenches: First Hand Accounts of Tank Warfare in the First World War, David Fletcher,
The History Press, 2009

General:

Beyond the Call of Duty: Bravery and Heroism in World War I, (in assocation with the National Archives),
Peter Hicks, Wayland, 2013

The First World War 1914–1918, Pam Robson,
Wayland, 2013

War in the Trenches: Remembering World War One,
Peter Hicks, Wayland, 2013

Resources

Imperial War Museum:
Lambeth Road, London, SE1 6HZ
Tel: 020 7416 5374
www.iwm.org.uk

Imperial War Museum North:
The Quays, Trafford Wharf Road, Trafford Park,
Manchester, M17 1TZ
Tel: 0161 836 4000
www.iwm.org.uk

BBC History Online:
www.bbc.co.uk/history/worldwars/wwone

The Great War:
www.pitt.edu/~pugachev/greatwar/ww1.html
Large site dedicated to World War I with a massive
collection of links as well.

Hellfire Corner:
www.fylde.demon.co.uk/welcome.htm
Tom Morgan's excellent collection of articles
and features on World War I.

Index